The LifeBreath® Book

Radiant Health
Mental Clarity
Emotional Peace
Spiritual Fulfillment

Attained through

**Knowledge of the
Powerful Science
of Breathwork**

&

**Practicing
The Inner Art
Of Breathing
&
Conscious Intention**

by
Beth Ann Bielat

Published by *LifeBreath*® *Institute*

Copyright
© 2004 Beth Bielat. All rights reserved. No part of this publication may be reproduced, stored in a retrieval system, or transmitted in any form or by any means, electronic, mechanical, photocopying, recording, or otherwise, without the prior written consent of Beth Bielat and The LifeBreath Institute, P.O. Box 262, Casco, ME 04015.

Cover Photo Shannon Bielat

Typesetting & Cover Design The Write Stuff, 24 Portland Street, Fryeburg, Maine 04037

Printed in conjunction with Goose River Press, 3400 Friendship Road, Waldoboro, Maine 04572

ISBN 1-930648-87-1

Library of Congress Control Number: 2004104370

Caution:
This book is in no way a replacement for necessary medical treatment or a prescription for health problems. Always consult your doctor before beginning any exercise program.

Dedication

*This book is dedicated to the thousands of people
who have inspired me by their experiences with
the power and the spirit of LifeBreath ...
and to those who have not yet found it, but will.*

Contents

Introduction
- In Appreciation 7
- Preface 9
- Introduction – My Story 10
- How to Use This Book 13

Section I – Breathwork & Chi 15
- A Brief History of Breathwork 16
- Conscious Breathing and the LifeBreath Technique (PEMS)
  - A Multi-Purpose Tool 18
  - General Benefits to Better Breathing 19
  - Natural Everyday Breathing 23
  - The Nine Keys to Healthy Normal Breathing 20
  - The Science of Breath – Understanding the Basic
    Scientific Mechanics of Breathing 23
    - Anatomy of Breathing 25
- Chi
  - Understanding Fundamental Life Force Energy and Breath ... 31
  - Benefits and Insights from Full Everyday Diaphragmatic
    Breathing and The LifeBreath Technique 38
    - **P**hysical 43
    - **E**motional 47
    - **M**ental 55
    - **S**piritual 59
- Chakra Basics 64
  - The Seven Major Chakras
    I, II, III, IV, V, VI, VII 65
- Common Restricted Breathing Patterns in Everyday Life
  - Why We Learned Restricted Breathing Patterns
    in the First Place 90
- Restricted Breathing Patterns 101 93
- Breathwork with Special Populations 100

Section II – The LifeBreath Technique 105
- How It's Done 111
- When It's Done 113
- Where It's Done 115
- What May Happen During a Session 116
  - **P**hysically 116
  - **M**entally 119

   Emotionally 121
   Spiritually 124
   After a Session 125
  LifeBreath as a Tool to Meet the Needs of Special Populations 127
  LifeBreath Breathing Analysis 129
  Transformational Tools Used During a LifeBreath Session 135
   The Breath 135
   Setting an Intention 135
   Music 135
   Instruction During the Session 146
   Body Mapping and Touch Points 137
   Affirmations for Breathing 141
   Affirmations for Integrating the Breath 142
   Toning 144
   Reiki 145
   Tapping 145
   Prayer and Conscious Intention 146

Section III — Life Exercises
Exercises that Change the Way We Live 147
   Conscious Breathing Techniques 148
   Cleansing Breath 148
   Oxygenating Health Breath 148
   Relaxation 148
   Yin Yang Breathing 149
   Kundalini 150
   Ha Breath 151
   Boogie Breathing 151
   Belly Only Breath 153
   Heart Only Breath 153
   Toning Exercises 154
  LifeBreath Style Tai Chi / Chi Kung 156
   Standing Meditation and Rooting 157
   Discovering Chi 159
   Standing Meditation and Circulating Chi
    Through the Microcosmic Orbit 160
   Zap: Discovering Chi 161
   Trasmitting Chi 162
   Awakening Chi 163
   Gathering Earth Energy 165
   Gathering Universal Energy 170
   Trunk Rolls 172
   Cleansing the Lungs 174
   Cleansing Your Aura 176
  Meditation 177
   Alpha Induction 179

A Few Favorite Meditations and Creative Visualization Exercises . 181
    Triune Breath and Meditation 181
    Third Eye Breathing 182
    Affirmation Meditation 183
    A Little Piece of Heaven 183
    Calling Forth Spiritual Guidance 183
    Angel Massage 183
    Body Scanning 183
    Chakra Alignment and Attunement 184
Light Bulb Moment Exercises...Aha's 189
    Forgiveness Exercises 189
    Letter to God and Back 191
    What's Up Exercise 191
    Funeral Exercise 192
    A Letter to Someone You Love 192
    Paradigm Shifting 192
    More Paradigm Shifting 194
    $100.00 Exercise 195
    A Letter to Someone On Your Shoulders 195
    Affirmation Exercise 196
    Rocking Chair Test 197
    Code of Ethics 197
    Attribute Exercise 198
    Shape Shifting with a Partner 198
    Smile Exercise 198
    Mirror Exercise 198
    Moving Communication 199
    River of Time 199
    Ever Changing Committment 200
    Candle Ceremony 200
    Muscle Testing 201
    Goal Setting 201

Bibliography 204

Tapes from LifeBreath Institute 206

About the Auther 208

Contact Information 208

In Appreciation

This project has blossomed at the hands of the faithful supporters of LifeBreath. To all those wonderful folks whom I have met for either a brief encounter or who have stayed in my life for decades – each and every one of you is in my heart and you have inspired me to write this book. I have watched you transform during a simple one hour class of chi kung. I have also seen you experience cathartic change through conscious intention and LifeBreath Techniques. Each time I meet another single soul who is open to this magic, I am in awe and I honor and appreciate you.

Thank you to all the members of Bushido Karate Dojo and Fitness Center and LifeBreath Institute, my extended family, because you have been at the core of my life. Thank you to all the "outside classes" in Maine like Poland Spring Inn, Camp Sunshine and Point Sebago. To the school systems and recreation departments where we teach Martial Arts and Fitness – thank you for sharing your children and bringing great joy into my life for the last two decades. Thank you to all the wonderful people in New Jersey who have been faithful followers over the years. To all the new wonderful friends and supporters in Florida, I feel as though we've been together for many lives. Thank you for making me feel so welcome. Each of you are great teachers – I have learned so much.

Thank you to everyone who helped with the actual writing of this book.

Thanks, Lisa Magiera (and her beautiful family), for being my right hand woman and for being there for whatever I needed you to attend to, from editing our newsletter to taking care of BKD for six months each year. You have a gift for both teaching and learning. Thanks to Kerrie Toole for you wonderful knowledge of writing and your intuitive wisdom and discernment between proper writing styles and my style. (And your sense of humor to help me through). You are extremely intelligent, with a perfect blend of softness. Nat Beal, your editing and layout skills are wonderful and truly appreciated. Without you all, this project would have been nearly impossible.

I want to thank my family for all their support. First there are my siblings. We've been through a lot together and the ties that bind us are very strong and I love you so very much. My big brother Mark, thank you. You have been a critical guide, friend, mentor, and one of the biggest influences in my life. And to my sisters, Sue and Fran, thank you for always being there and loving me unconditionally. You all had a huge part in my upbringing. We made it through all the trials and tribulations of youth. Although you passed away early in my life, Mom and Dad, you were two of my greatest teachers and I still feel your love.

Then there is my in-law family. You have been wonderful. Mom and Dad, you have accepted me into your loving family from the beginning. Even before my own parents' passing, you have been parents, friends, and an inspiration to me. Thank you for being there. I have always felt at home, very loved and safe with you.

To my children, Sean and Shannon, I could never have dreamed of having such incredible love in my life. You have both made me very proud of you, not for your achievements or goals you have reached, but for the kind, loving and giving people you have turned out to be. You two have inspired me to do many of the things I do today. Sean, you help me keep a level head on my shoulders, see things as they are, and to stay grounded. Shannon, you keep me on the straight and narrow about being non-judgmental, standing my own ground, and staying balanced. Thank you for your continued support and love.

John, my husband, partner, soul mate, and biggest fan, what can I say? I believe that without you, none of this would have come to fruition at this point in my life. You make me feel like I can do anything! Your words of encouragement electrify me. When you tell me that I am smart or beautiful or I'm a great teacher, it goes right to my heart and I am revitalized. Your love and support have a magical influence for me and I want to thank you for your trust, love, confidence, time, balance, outdoor savvy, love of nature, teachings, inspirations, and loyalty. You are an incredible man. I'll always love you and I continue to be inspired by you.

I give thanks and praise to God each and every day. The power of the universe is both awesome and loving.

Preface

"And the Lord God formed man of the dust of the ground, and breathed into his nostrils the breath of life; and man became a living soul."
—**Genesis 2:7, King James Bible**

For thousands of years, sages of ancient civilizations have used the powerful science and inner art of breathing to master the human conditions of fear and illness and for attaining spiritual enlightenment. They discovered that through breathing, they had direct access to the divine energy of the universe. Breathwork is the very key to our physical, emotional, mental, and spiritual well being. The fact that one must breathe to live makes breathing synonymous with life. As we improve our breathing, we improve our lives. The simple act of conscious breathing helps bridge the gap between our human frailties and the divine. Watch a healthy baby breathe – you'll see a perfect breath: connected, diaphragmatic, full, and relaxed. As we grow older, we actually un-learn and restrict our breathing and, in order to obtain radiant health, we must go back to that baby's breath. Understanding and practicing breathing may possibly be one of the most important things you do in this lifetime.

"At its best (breath) brings immortality; at the very least it profits towards long life. If the body is sick, meditate on the breath to work on the illness and the sickness will be healed promptly: when the mind wills the breath energy into the limbs, it works like magic." —Sung-Shan, Taoist Sage

"If I had to limit my advice on healthier living to just one tip, it would be simply to learn how to breathe correctly. From my own experience and from working with patients, I have come to believe that proper breathing is the master key to good health." —Dr. Andrew Weil, MD

*"Breathe well, live well.
Breathe poorly, live poorly."*
—Dr. Tom Goode, International Breath Institute

"Partial Breathing is Partial Living"
—Ancient Chinese Adage

In this book we will explore magical lessons in life and breath.

Introduction

My Story

I spent the first eighteen years of my life growing up in middle class, suburban New Jersey. My first memory of conscious breathing was when I was about eight years old. I was an avid swimmer, a water child, and I used to spend countless hours in our community pool. I would go to the deep end of the pool and "bob." I would close my eyes, take a huge breath in, force myself to the bottom with arms raised up over head, hit the bottom, push off to the top while exhaling, flapping my arms downward, then start all over again. There was a gentle but powerful rhythm and I would literally do this for hours. I didn't realize it then, but I was "breathing" and putting myself into altered states of awareness. I remember a dream-like state, feeling as though I was flying and almost formless. I felt an overwhelming sense of peace and connection that I later found through conscious breathing techniques and, ultimately, LifeBreath.

I started martial arts when I was nine. Breathing was often mentioned during classes and we practiced a few simple breath patterns associated with martial application and creating internal and physical power. When I was old enough to study myself, I became interested in meditation, simple breathing techniques and I continued my studies in karate and then tai chi and chi kung. The breathing modalities brought a sense of calm, but they were very subtle and I practiced only occasionally.

In my twenties and early thirties I was married, living in Maine, via New Mexico, and had two young children. I was a stay at home mom and had a full time career (or two or three) that included teaching martial arts, fitness, and wellness. I was very busy between family, helping my husband run his construction business, and teaching. I was basically happy, but I had an inner sense of longing for something "more" in my spiritual life. Life was good, but I knew I was missing a big piece of the puzzle in the grand scheme of it all.

When I was in my early thirties, I was introduced to "Transformational Breathing," the predecessor to LifeBreath. One of my karate student's mother invited me to do a session and she told me that she thought I would love this breathwork, so we booked a private session and boy, was she right! Going into the session, I honestly thought that I had *done* breathwork and there wasn't all that much new to learn. I also thought that I basically had my "stuff" together, later to find out that there were whole new levels of breathwork, peace, joy, and love that I had not yet experienced. I was open enough to follow directions and BREATHE! *(And that's all I ask for when I facilitate others now.)*

To be perfectly honest, the experience absolutely, positively, unequivocally ... knocked my socks off! I remember feeling SO many emotions, but very differently than ever before. The feelings were deep and extremely vivid. I could FEEL them in my body and I sensed that I was experiencing them from a soul perspective. My session was also more physical than anything I had ever experienced. At one point, I felt as though my body was vibrating, almost like one of those paint shakers in a hardware store. I had to open my eyes and look – and – it was! My entire body was vibrating with life force. It felt like someone had plugged me into a fire truck hose and put it on full blast. The amount of chi (energy) I was feeling was quite overwhelming and actually made me laugh and laugh until I cried with joy. I found the tool that I was searching for. I found my spiritual connection. I was on the path of spiritual revelation. I believe I got further spiritually in that one session than I thought I would get in this lifetime. Years of meditation, reading, and searching were no match for *Breath*. Needless to say, I was hooked, so I began doing Breath sessions on my own every day. I Breathed for two years straight, every single day.

One of my favorite sessions during that time was about my parents. Although they had both passed away years prior, during that session I was surely with them. To make a long story short, we had some serious healing that needed to be done (alcoholic Dad, strained family relationships, etc). The session is difficult to put to words because it was so "Big," but during the session it felt as though I left my body and I was a *being of light.* My parents were also beings of light and we were surrounded by the universe, darkness and stars, and an overwhelming sense of oneness with all. Our three energies combined and our light forces joined one another and it felt as though a thousand angels came upon us, surrounded and embraced us, and poured more love into us than I thought was heavenly possible. When I came back into my physical body, I heard (or more appropriately, felt) the words, "It's all right now. Everything is all right now." Years, perhaps lifetimes, had been healed and made "all right" by this experience. I realized in those moments that my parents were also spiritual beings on their own path which intertwined with mine. They had always done the best they could and they always loved me and I always loved them. Once back into reality, I felt loved, overwhelmed, and joyful. That feeling has stuck.

During the first few months I was doing my beloved Breathwork, my friends and family weren't sure if I was "losing it." (*losing "what" I didn't know*). John, my husband, thought I might be going through some weird life changes. My kids thought I was really mushy. Friends started seeing strange changes in me, I didn't want to drink and party, and I wanted everyone to experience what I was experiencing – physical energy, mental and emotional elation, and spiritual bliss.

One day after a breath session, I came downstairs to find John in the kitchen.

I was still very physically buzzed and very emotional, feeling loved and loving. I began to explain to John how I was feeling and he was trying to understand. Up to this point he was not interested in doing a Breath session. He was turned sideways to me and I placed my (vibrating) hands on his heart and directly behind his heart on his back. I said, "Can't you feel that?" At that moment, John's knees buckled and he began to cry. We embraced that moment and our lives together changed forever. The next day he did his first breath session and has been my soul partner ever since.

I continued my studies in ancient breathwork, Chi Kung, Tai Chi, personal training, energy work, meditation, and holistic health. I immediately trained to become a facilitator, then a trainer of facilitators of Transformational Breath. A few years later, I created LifeBreath Institute to teach, train, and spread the joy that my breathwork has gifted me. LifeBreath Techniques can be miraculous and I pledge to share them with you.

Because of Breathwork, my life feels directed and yet flowing. I feel balanced, peaceful, loving, and joyful. Because of LifeBreath, I am more intuitive and I feel closer to my spirit. I knew from the very beginning that I was being called to share LifeBreath with as many people as possible.

How to Use This Book

This book has been written in three sections.

In section I, **Breathwork & Chi,** we look at the fundamentals about breathing and energy, the benefits of the LifeBreath Technique and full diaphragmatic breathing, and universal truths about physical, emotional, mental, and spiritual well-being.

Section II, **LifeBreath**, is a detailed look at the LifeBreath Technique. Many testimonials are shared to help you deeply feel the power of this modality.

Lastly, Part III, **LifeExercise**, includes a resource guide for exercises that can profoundly transform your life as they did mine.
Please use them!!

Use this book to help transform your life by
first **learning,** *and then* **doing.**

You have my promise and pledge that when you begin using the
LifeBreath technique and the other tools in this book
your life will begin to change for the better.

Section I

Breathwork

&

Chi

A Brief History of Breathwork

Breathwork has been used for thousands of years for improving physical and mental health and longevity, as well as for emotional healing and spiritual enlightenment. The ancient civilizations of Greece, India and China each formalized systems of breathwork for physical, emotional, mental, and spiritual well-being. Centuries of practice are the foundation of today's breathing systems.

There is a life energy that *rides in on* our breath. The ancient people throughout the world knew of this life force and used it to manifest wholeness and wellness in their everyday lives. The Hindus called this energy "prana," the very feeling of God in the body. Chinese sages called it "chi," meaning life, spirit, and air. In Hebrew, "Rauch" means both breath and life force. In ancient Greece, the principals of breathing were what they believed sustained the life of the universe. Inspiration and spirit have their root word in Latin as "to breathe." Spirit, Breath, and air in Greek are all referred to as "psyche pnuema" and the Romans called it "spiritus."

The oldest societies in the world learned to harness breath as a means to *inspire* their very body and soul.

Not until the 1970's was Breathwork introduced into modern America with a strong emphasis on spreading it as a viable tool for wellness. Dr. Stan Grof, MD developed *Holotropic Breathwork* to assist his patients in attaining altered states of mind and holistic wellness, and Jacquelyn Small used *Integrative Breathwork* for addictive behavior modification. Leonard Orr created *Rebirthing* to assist in healing our first trauma, birth, so that we could move on and experience life from a different, healthier frame of mind. *Radiance Breathwork* is used today by the infamous Dr. Gay Hendricks, and Dr. Andrew Weil professes breathing with his clients for a variety of therapeutic exercises. Judith Kravitz and Tom Goode worked together and created *Transformational Breathing and Full Wave Breathing*, based on full diaphragmatic breathwork. These are at the roots of the LifeBreath system.

In the U.S. there has been resurgence in the practices of breathwork of India called *pranayama* from Yoga and of *Chi Kung* from China's Tai Chi. Native American practices, meditation modalities, and even fitness exercises like Pilates and weight training all include types of breathwork that have grown in popularity throughout the world because of their life giving properties.

The *LifeBreath Technique* and LifeBreath Institute were created in 1996 to expand peoples' knowledge of Breathwork and help create more peace, joy, and fulfillment, along with better health and longevity for its practitioners. The LifeBreath Institute teaches various techniques and breathing styles to aid in the healing and wellness of its students. The most powerful and profound technique we come to experience is called the *LifeBreath Technique* or just *"LifeBreath."* The LifeBreath Institute creates programs for mainstream Americans to grow, learn and flourish in breathwork, holistic health, transformation, and personal power.

There are literally hundreds of different breathing techniques that vary in form and style. Some are very similar and others are at opposing ends of a large spectrum comprised of extremely physical and active breaths to very subtle, inactive breaths. There is no one right way to breathe, but a more effective way for a given situation or desired outcome. Different activities warrant different breaths. Your natural breathing patterns are unique to you, they are like a fingerprint that tells the story of your life. Once again, we are focused on going back to the way we breathed as healthy babies to help create optimal radiant health in the body, mind, and spirit.

**By changing the patterns in your breathing,
you can change the patterns in your life.**

The LifeBreath Technique can bring you to an elevated state of mind/body/soul that will continue to expand as your knowledge and practice expands.

Conscious Breathing and the LifeBreath Technique

A Multi-Purpose Tool

PEMS

Physical
Emotional
Mental
Spiritual

"You can use conscious breathing and willingness in each and every moment to balance your energy, face a challenge, love yourself and others, and release your creativity."
—Sajata

"Can you master your wandering mind and realize the Original Unit; can you adjust your breath, cultivate essential energy, and sustain the suppleness of a newborn with no cares?" —Lao Zi, Chinese Philosopher

General Benefits from Better Breathing

Physical
LifeBreath conscious Breathing techniques are being used to create physical health, energy, and endurance, enhance physical performance, prevent, manage, and heal physical problems, and assist in graceful aging. Breathwork has been used to manage pain and help in peoples' healing processes. Sexual energy can also be enhanced through breathwork.

Emotional
Stress and tension reduction are two very powerful reasons to focus on one's breath. Emotional mastery and well-being are directly connected to our breathing patterns. We can not have mastery over our emotions without focusing on our breath. Through LifeBreath, one can learn how to let go of the past, stop worrying about the future, and truly live in the moment in a place with more joy, peace, and happiness.

Mental
Breathwork helps create clarity, focused concentration, and enhanced mental/physical performance. Breathwork helps create the "relaxation response" that occurs through our mind to help relax us.

Spiritual
Breathwork is not religious, but it is spiritual in nature, and can help you connect to your spirituality. Many ancient civilizations and modern cultures use breathwork for spiritual connection and psycho-spiritual transformation.

Natural Everyday Breathing

The Lifebreath Technique and many other conscious breathing tools are used for what I call "special occasion breathing," in that we initially only use these techniques during training sessions. Once aware of and comfortable with Breathwork, we ultimately use these modalities to make our lives better *all the time*, not just when we are performing the exercises.

Different breathing patterns elicit different responses in your body, emotions and attitude. Learning to breathe better in general enhances your life and keeps you *more alive*. Your breathing will change according to what you are doing and how you are feeling. Your breath will change with your moods and your current personal paradigms. You have a natural breath pattern when you are talking and another when you are walking, one when you are happy and another when you are sad. When you move and exercise, your breath can be conscious or subconscious. Your mood is also subconsciously and consciously transformed by your breathing pattern.

To improve your life become a habitual full belly breather...
Your energy will increase, your attitude will change for
the better and your spirit will be uplifted.

Good, natural *"Everyday Breathing"* is usually done...

Through the nose
Diaphragmatically (using the diaphragm muscle) and
Fully, in the lower belly, diaphragm and chest
In a relaxed manner

Baby's "The Perfect Breath"

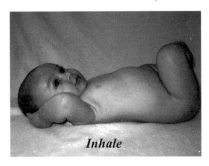
Inhale

Exhale

—Photos by Lisa and Eric Magiera

The Nine Keys to Healthy Normal Breathing

Optimal Health, Longevity, and Inner Harmony = Chi (Energy) Flow = Healthy Normal Breathing = Practice and Intention

Breathing techniques govern body and mind. By regulating body, mind, and breath, you will be able to manage your life energy, or chi, and lead it smoothly and naturally. Chi and breathing are mutually related and can not be separated.

In the ancient practice of Chi Kung Breathwork there are fundamental components to normal, natural, every day breathing that are expanded upon below. These components are crucial, as they assist in creating optimal health and well-being.

1. & 2. Calm and Quiet
When the mind is calm the breath is quiet.
When the mind is calm and peaceful we are able to regulate our breathing.
Unless you are doing "special occasion breathing," the breath is calm and quiet.
Keep breathing quietly, in order to relax and be peaceful.

3. Slender
When you naturally breathe, visualize it as a tiny stream.
It is smooth, natural, and slender.
This is a key to deeper levels of meditation, an alpha state, and relaxation.

4. & 5. Deep and Full
When you breathe deeply, draw the air down in the abdomen and up into the chest.
Visualize drawing air in by moving the diaphragm down rather than by just expanding the chest upward.
Do not expand to the maximum lung capcity, only to approximately 70 to 80 percent so that your muscles stay relaxed.

6. Long
Do not hold your breath, but lengthen your breath by slowing it down.
This will make you more relaxed and your mind more meditative and quiet.
Slowing your breath down helps slow heart rate and requires less oxygen.

7. & 8. Continuous and Smooth
Natural and continuous – no stagnation *(unless performing special training)*
If you stop and hold your breath your body will tense. Continuous and smooth breathing helps keep you focused and more centered.

9. Uniform
Only by managing your emotions will you be able to keep your breath uniform.
Your breath is affected by your emotions and, in order to attain uniformity, you must regulate your emotional mind.

(Taken, in part, from <u>The Healing Promise of Qi,</u> by Roger Jahnke, O.M.D.)

As you read this book, please remind yourself to breathe this way.

Allow this to become your natural breathing pattern by becoming aware of your breathing and consciously shifting it towards the nine keys to healthy normal breathing.

Practice and intention will help you master your good healthy breathing and will help make it a new habit.

Wave Breath

1.2.3. Inhale Fully   4. Relax the Exhale

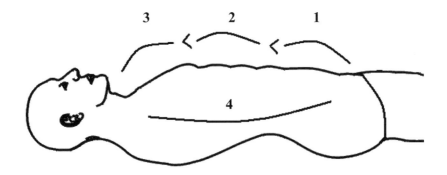

The Science of Breath

Understanding the Basics of Breathing

It is important to understand the basic science, anatomy, and physiology behind breathing so that you can more fully experience and master your own breath.

The respiratory system consists of the nasal cavity, pharynx, larynx, and trachea, and the bronchi, bronchioles, and the alveoli within the lungs. The system permits gaseous exchange between the external environment and the blood.

The respiratory system has four basic scientific functions:

1. Provide oxygen to the bloodstream and remove carbon dioxide.
2. Sound production (vocalization) as expired air passes over the vocal cords.
3. Assist in abdominal compressions during urination, defecation, and childbirth.
4. Through coughing and sneezing, it acts as a component of a protection reflex.

The respiratory system is also a place where life force enters the body, riding up on your inhalation, and during the exhale, the spent life energy is released.

There are two phases associated with breathing or ventilation, the inhale and the exhale. During the inhale, the diaphragm and intercostal muscles around the ribcage contract. The diaphragm moves downward and increases the volume of the chest cavity and, along with the intercostal and abdominal muscles, allows the ribcage and lungs to expand. The negative atmosphere that is created rushes the air into the alveoli walls where the external exchange of oxygen and carbon dioxide occurs. So, inspiration occurs as the intrathoracic pressure is reduced through the contraction of the diaphragm, the external intercostal muscles, and the movement of air into the lungs.

During the exhale stage (expiration), the diaphragm, intercostal, and abdominal muscles relax and the diaphragm and rib cage rebound. The air pressure increases in the lungs, forcing the air out as the inspiratory muscles are relaxed.

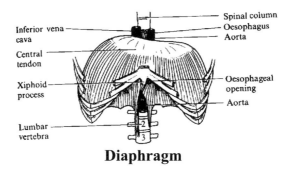

Diaphragm

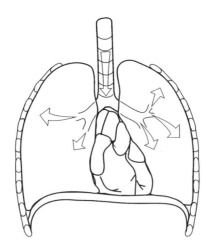

Inspiration

Contraction of diaphragm and external intercostals

    Expansion of rib cage and inflation of lungs
    Decrease in intrapulmonic pressure

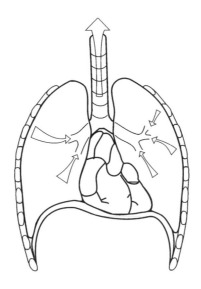

Expiration

Relaxation of diaphragm and external intercostals

    Recoil of rib cage and partial deflation of lungs
    Increase in intrapulmonic pressure

Anatomy of Breathing

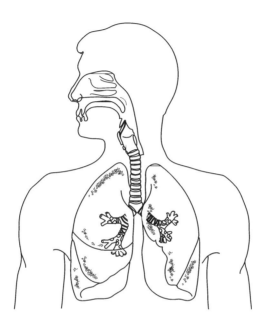

"When a breath is taken, air passes in through the nostrils, through the nasal passages, into the pharynx, through the larynx, down the trachea, into one of the main bronchi, then into smaller broncial tubules, through even smaller broncioles, and into a microscopic air sac called an alveolus. It is here that external respiration occurs. Simply put, it is the exhange of oxygen and carbon dioxide between the air and the blood in the lungs. Blood enters the lungs via the pulmonary arteries. It then proceeds through arterioles and into the alveolar capillaries. Oxygen and carbon dioxide are exchanged between blood and the air. This blood then flows out of the alveolar capillaries, through venuoles, and back to the heart via the pulmonary veins."

—www.stemnet.nf.ca

Internal respiration is basically the exchange of gasses between the blood in the capillaries and the body's cells.

The Nose and Nasal Cavity

As air enters through the nose, the nose and nasal passages have three basic purposes of moistening, filtering, and warming the air before it reaches the lungs. This area also responds to volatile chemical particles, when sensing odors, and assists in voice phonetics as a resonating chamber.

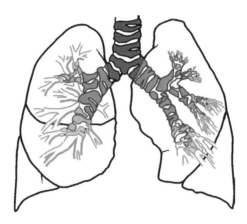

The Pharynx and Larynx

Also known as the throat, the pharynx leads into the larynx or voice box. The pharynx is a funnel-shaped passageway about five inches in length connecting the oral and nasal cavities to the esophagus and trachea. The pharynx also has digestive functions. The larynx is an organ consisting of both muscle and cartilage, located between the pharynx and the trachea. The larynx has two functions. It prevents food or liquid from entering the trachea and lungs during swallowing, and permits passage of air while breathing. Secondly, it produces sound vibration. There is a diaphragm located here that billows as we breathe.

The Lungs

The lungs are a paired respiratory organ within the thoracic cavity separated by the mediastinum. It contains pulmonary vessels and bronchial trees for gaseous exchange.

The Trachea and the Bronchial Tree

This is the portion of the respiratory system that transports ventilated air between the larynx in the neck and the respiratory sacs within the lungs. The trachea, or windpipe, is a tube approximately 4½ inches long, that leads to the bronchi and lungs. The trachea also serves as a filter system that traps mucus and foreign objects and moves them up through the pharynx where they then can be expelled.

The bronchial tree is where the narrowing trachea divides into two cartilage rings and enters the lungs in smaller groups called bronchioles. The bronchioles divide many times, getting thinner and thinner walls ending in alveoli.

The Alveoli

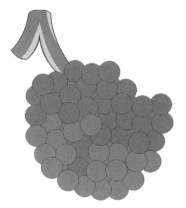

These minute air capsules within the lungs, grouped in grape-like bunches, are each only a cell thick. The estimated 350 million alveoli per lung provide an enormous surface area (about 760 square feet) for the diffusion of gases between the lung and blood. The exchange of oxygen and carbon dioxide within the circulatory system occurs through the thin-walled, moistened alveoli, making them the functional center of the respiratory system. Pulmonary capillaries surrounding alveoli have such small diameters that red blood cells travel in single file as they are pumped around the alveoli. During the gaseous exchange, oxygen diffuses through the alveolar walls and attaches to the hemoglobin of red blood cells in the adjacent capillaries, while carbon dioxide diffuses from the blood through the capillary and alveolar walls to enter the alveoli.

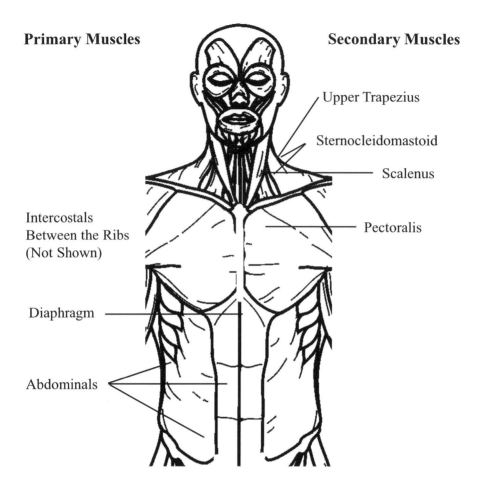

Primary Muscles — Intercostals Between the Ribs (Not Shown), Diaphragm, Abdominals

Secondary Muscles — Upper Trapezius, Sternocleidomastoid, Scalenus, Pectoralis

Primary and Secondary Respiratory Muscles

Primary Breathing Muscles
Diaphragm, intercostals, abdominals

We breathe every minute of every day. The primary muscles for breathing are the diaphragm, intercostals, and abdominals. When we breathe diaphragmatically, the diaphragm moves downward on the inhale and moves upward on the exhale. The diaphragm also expands and contracts during the inhale and exhale, respectfully. It massages all the surrounding organs, which gives them exercise and increases blood circulation through them and, thus, more oxygen is available to the organs. The diaphragm is attached to the heart, so when we diaphragmatically breathe, we exercise the heart as well. When we breathe more deeply, the diaphragm lowers, elongating the lungs, stretching and extending the dimension of the diphragm, causing the lower ribs and lower lungs to expand. The fact that the organs massage the heart is great news for those who suffer from heart disease. Other organs benefit from diaphragmatic breathing and many supportive studies are being done that correlate good health with good diaphragmatic breathing.

Diaphragmatic breathing also facilitates the greatest diffusion of oxygen and carbon dioxide. The lower lungs have a higher density of blood capillaries surrounding the alveoli and there is a more efficient oxygen exchange in the lower lungs than higher. Again, diaphragmatic breathing is synonymous with better overall health.

Secondary Breathing Muscles
Scalenus, Pectoralis, Sternocleidomastoid, Trapezius

The secondary muscles for breathing are the scalenus (in front of the neck attached to the upper rib), the pectoralis (in the chest), the sternocleidomastoid (just behind the ear to the sternum and clavicle), and the upper trapezius (from the base of the skull to the top of the shoulder blades). The primary muscles are large and strong and are built for long term breathing (which we do every minute of every day, about 22,000 times each day). The smaller, secondary muscles are just that … secondary, only to be used when needed for extra effort, emergencies, and to support the primary muscles.

Our problems begin when we reverse the roles of primary and secondary muscles, as our breathing becomes restricted and we do not use our full lung capacity. Most people breathe shallowly and/or restrictively, relying on the secondary muscles to do much of the work. The secondary muscles are the same ones that are engaged during the fight or flight response and during times of stress, which I will explain later. When we reverse the roles of the primary and secondary respiratory muscles we become tired and oxygen deficient. When we are very shallow breathers, the carbon dioxide may not be expelled fully and we can literally begin to poison our own bodies with the toxins. Also, the secondary muscles are smaller and they tire easily. The restrictive breathing patterns that we have accumulated throughout our lives, that have caused us NOT to breathe fully and smoothly, will be perpetuated. Overuse of the secondary muscles in breathing is a physical manifestation of the common societal syndrome of tightening the belly, the fast paced superficial lifestyle of fight or flight, stress, and increased physical and emotional trauma.

The LifeBreath Technique retrains our breathing patterns to, for example, go lower into the abdomen or higher into the chest, depending upon where we are restricted. LifeBreath also modifies breathing to allow the body to use the primary muscles, causing the diaphragm to extend downward and outward, which allows more oxygen and energy transfer into the bloodstream through the alveoli.

So ... why is it important to understand the science behind breathing?

Every biological function uses oxygen directly or indirectly. The very act of breathing stimulates and massages our internal organs, the diaphragm, and the abdominal muscles. The oxygen in the lungs cleanses and revitalizes the entire organ system. Approximately 70% of our toxins are released through exhalation (not perspiration or elimination) and 75% of our energy is taken in through inhalation (not food nor water). Fragile and dysfunctional breathing can weaken the immune system and break down the body's ability to function at its peak.

Understanding the anatomy and physiology of breathing assists our process in healthy breathing. It just makes sense that effective diaphragmatic breathing brings in more oxygen and expels more carbon dioxide. The actual movement massages all our organs, including the heart, and the process encourages a healthier state in the body/mind. So when you learn the science of where and why your breath travels throughout the body, it encourages and leverages you to become a better breather. ***Knowledge is power.***

Full Conscious Breathing: A Cure All?

By breathing diaphragmatically and fully, the oxygen is brought down into the lower lungs where the most contact with blood occurs so that the oxygen can be delivered through the body for every cell to use. The lower lungs can incur a rate of blood flow more than ten times higher than the upper lungs. This is one very important factor in why belly breathing has so many benefits **P**hysically, **E**motionally, **M**entally and **S**piritually (**PEMS**). Specifically, when the cells are oxygenated more efficiently, the energy level is raised. We feel more energetic and balanced physically and emotionally, often immediately, from taking deeper breaths. In part, this is also why exercise is so good for us. We more fully oxygenate, stress is reduced, endorphins are released, and we feel rejuvenated and full of vim and vigor.

- Did you know that when your brain does not get enough oxygen, it steals it from other organs?
- And wouldn't it make sense that the other organs would not operate as effectively and efficiently without the oxygen they need? ...
- And that the entire body would begin to operate in an oxygen deficient mode?...
- And that the entire PEMS system would be affected?...
- Couldn't it just be possible that health, on all levels, is affected by the way you breathe?

YES! YES! AND *YES!*

Chi
Understanding Fundamental Life Force Energy and Breath

Chi is living energy. It is the force behind all of nature that causes the planets to maintain their orbit, the tides to rise and fall, and trees to grow. It is the energy matrix that directs the evolutionary process of a single cell duplicating and then being guided into an embryo that creates a frog or a horse or a person. Chi is physical energy and it is also consciousness. It is the essence behind everything — people, places, and things, and the cause and effect that influences all events.

The health and well-being of an individual, a household, a continent, or the world is contingent upon the chi that flows to and from and in and out of that entity.

> **People can consciously learn how to discover, gather, circulate, purify, direct, conserve, store, transform, dissolve, and transmit chi through regulating their body posture or movement, their breathing, and their consciousness or thoughts.**

We are all born with certain amounts and different kinds of energy called birth chi or original chi. This is what makes us who we are. I call this whole concept "spiritual DNA," all the personalities, physical-alities (*I make up words*) emotion-alities *(that one too)* and spirituality that we are born with.

Although we are born with dispositions and birth energy, it is through our experiences that we receive environmental, family, and social energy. We can also learn how to consciously work with our chi. Our experiences and our consciousness begin to form who we are.

Try this exercise to *feel* your own chi…

> *Hold your arms out in front of you, about shoulder height, and then, very quickly, make a tight fist then release the fist and zap your fingers out. Do this about thirty times, fast, with your palms down. Then flip your palms up and zap another thirty quick times. Now, form a ball with your hands and arms in front of you like your holding a basketball ready to throw, hands about six inches apart. Totally relax your hands and arms. Close your eyes and feel the energy in your hands. Move the ball slightly smaller and larger and feel the magnetic pull. You may feel tingling, heat, or sense an energy field between your hands.* (See Zap Exercise, page 161)

In order to stay alive, we must *consciously* bring chi into our bodies in three basic ways.

The first way we draw energy to us is through the food we eat. Quality ***does*** matter. Even those of us with just basic knowledge about nutrition surely understand that the fresher and more organic foods are, the better they are for us because they have better and more chi. Cupcakes don't have the same chi as a head of lettuce. A head of lettuce that is a week old does not have the same chi as the one picked from your home grown garden. Anything processed, microwaved, canned or frozen, or filled with food dyes and pesticides, does not have the same chi it had when it was fresh, straight from Mother Nature.

The second way we bring chi into us is through the water we drink. Watching the sale of bottled water skyrocket over the last few years, I'm sure we all realize that pure water has better chi than chlorinated, recycled city water. Again, quality.

My hometown in Maine is located next to Poland Springs, where the famous bottling company sends water around the world. The history of Poland Springs is very interesting. In the 1800's people began drinking from a spring on their travels through the area. They found that they began to feel more energetic and it seemed to cure many ailments. Over time, word got out about the healing properties of the water. They began bottling the water and shipping it out all over the world. The area became a vacation getaway. In the early 1900's, people of fame and fortune traveled and vacationed at the Poland Spring Inn. Still today, people from all over come to stay at Poland Springs. They come to experience the "good chi," the water and the beauty the area has to offer. *Now we're starting to understand that quality is essential.*

The third way we bring in chi is the most immediate, the most abundant, and will be our focus. It's through **BREATHING!** Each breath we take in carries upon it vibrations of energy. We eat three to six meals per day, drink about eight glasses of water a day, but we breathe about 22,000 times a day!

**The quality, quantity, location, rhythm, and patterns
of breathing directly affect our chi flow physically,
emotionally, mentally, and spiritually.**

Very few people realize that the quality of their breathing is not only extremely important but essential on every level of life. In fact, your breathing is one of the most important things you do each day. We can go for a while without water, a little longer without food, but we can not go very long without breathing!

Most people figure that one day they "get born" and begin breathing. And one day they "get dead" and stop breathing. The *quality* of their breathing may be totally overlooked. In order to live optimally, we must look at the quality of our breathing.

But it's even more than this ...

**Changing the quality, quantity, style, and intention
of your breath will absolutely change your life.**

More About Chi

When everything is flowing well in our lives on all different levels, our chi is flowing too. Chi flows through the body many different ways. Put simply, Chi flows through us, to us, and from us. It flows on vein-like currents throughout our bodies called meridians. It also radiates from us and around us on different levels called auras. Our energy harbors in different areas in our body like a giant filing cabinet. These energy vortexes and nerve plexuses are called chakra (pronounced shock-ra or chak-ra).

These meridians and chakras are not imaginary things, they just can't be seen by most human eyes, much like radio and TV waves.

Let's look at the flow of energy and how it generally affects us. In a perfect world, with a perfect life, where everything is just "ducky," chi flows radiantly and abundantly through the entire body system *and then some.* However, for most of us, we perceive life has dealt some not-so-perfect pieces and that affects us, our chi, our life force.

From our personal paradigm, when something bothers us and we have to deal with it, even with the best tools, it affects our thoughts and our emotions. Because our bodies and minds are so interconnected, every negative thought and negatively perceived event registers in our body as negative chi. This automatically affects our physical body, and we may become *uneasy* in our energy flow and thus cause dis-ease, physically, emotionally, mentally, and spiritually.

As we deal with life's everyday happenings, trauma, stress, grief, happiness and joy, it affects every cell in our body. Each person has different levels of tolerance for how much ill effects it can handle. And each person can learn how best to intervene through experiencing and practicing different techniques and modalities he or she intuitively is drawn to.

When a lifetime of suppressed emotions begins to build up, it affects all aspects of life. The chi begins to move differently through the restricted body systems and the effects can eventually be seen and felt. It can be as simple as baggy eyes from stress and exhaustion, to cancer, heart attack, and even death. Why do you think so many illnesses manifest as we age? There is more and more research proving that diseases like cancer and heart disease **begin** on an energetic level (the thought process).

**Most importantly, every suppressed emotion,
every feeling of fear, and every negative thought
not only affects our chi flow, but it also negatively
affects and restricts our *breathing!***

**When we are relaxed and calm, peaceful
and loving, chi flows more radiantly.**

**When we are uptight and carry repressed unresolved
emotions, chi can be stagnant, restricted, and unbalanced.**

Chi Giving / Chi Robbing

Certain actions and thought forms recharge our energy, others drag our energy downward. We can be exhausted or energized, both literally and figuratively. People, thoughts, situations, events, being mad, sad, glad, fearful, happy, or resentful can either make us ill or can lift us up. The good news is that it is our choice and in our own hands to take charge of our energy.

+ Chi Giving

Sleep	R & R
Nature	Laughter
Love	Positive thinking
Positive paradigms	Self-confidence
Exercise	Learning
Healthy partners in life	Positive people
A fulfilling career	Lettuce-filled diet
Passion	A Life Mission
Healthy relationshiips	Breathing
Trust	

- Chi Robbing

Stress	Worry
Traffic	Distrust
Negative self talk	Overindulgence
Work we don't love	Vanity
Poor self image	Inactivity
Complacency	Unhealthy partners in life
Unhealthy relationships	Negative people
A JOB (just above broke)	A cupcake-filled diet
Boredom	Holding your Breath
Unhealthy addictions	

Unity Consciousness

There are ways of thinking that can create harmony, peace, and well-being, not only for us, but around us and for others. It's called unity thinking or unity consciousness. When you shift your thoughts from fear, scarcity, and an "everything happens TO me" attitude – to love, abundance, and an "I am the script writer of my life" attitude, your whole paradigm and energy flow begins to shift. Synchronistic occasions (those coincidences that aren't really coincidences) begin to take place, there is a shift in your life to an upward spiral and "life is good." Unity thinking is the opposite of fearful, polar thinking.

Here are some examples:

Fear Based	Love Based
I am afraid.	I am safe.
Everything happens TO me.	I am the script writer of my own destiny.
It's not my fault.	I take responsibility for my life.
Life is about suffering.	Life is about learning and loving.
Humans are bad by nature.	Humans are good by nature.
There isn't enough to go around.	Life is abundant and plentiful.
I am running away from the darkness.	I am heading toward the light.
There is no meaning to what happens.	Everything that happens moves me to a place closer to God, spirituality, and the truth.
I need others to make me feel whole.	I love others, but I am the only person that can make me feel complete.
My body (clothes, makeup, car, house) is who I am.	I am not my body. I am temporarily **in** this body.
My nature makes me nervous, anxious, or mean.	I am in charge of my thoughts and feelings.
I believe things are inevitable and inherited.	I create and attract what I believe in.

Preliminary Self Assessment of Chi Flow – A quick glimpse

Ample and Harmonious Chi	**Stagnant or Deficient Chi**
Little or no pain	Pain in the joints, muscles, etc.
Normal regular body temperature	Irregular body temperature
Normal regular pulse rate	Irregular or erratic pulse
Healthy appetite	Overeating / undereating
Well rested and good sleep patterns	Restlessness or sleeplessness
Good stamina and strength	Feeling fatigue or laziness
Feeling productive and energetic	Feeling stressed and tentative
Feeling creative and inspired	Sickness and disease
Feeling happy and peaceful	Feeling depressed and lethargic
Good healthy breathing	Difficulty breathing
Alert, good memory	Drifty and forgetful
Emotionally stable	Emotional instability
Pink, healthy, uncoated tongue	Pale or coated tongue
Bright eyes	Dull eyes
Regular digestive and bowel regulation	Irregular digestion and bowel regulation

By the way, ignoring the negative symptoms will not make them go away. If you're not on an upward spiral, action must be taken. If you do not act upon your own health and well-being, then you will learn a lesson in Karma about cause and effect and responsibility and irresponsibility.

Energy and Breath

According Einstein, matter and energy are interchangeable, mass can turn into energy and energy into mass. Breathing is synonymous with energy, thus, when we are accessing chi flow and breathing, we can open up constricted energy in the body through regulating our breathing, changing our posture, and working with our mind. There is an exchange of energy and mass. We can either change our mental state, our posture, or our breathing to alter the flow of chi.

Just becoming aware of holding your breath, especially during stressful times, is very helpful. When this occurs – BREATHE!

Becoming a full diaphragmatic breather is the next step, learning to bring the breath (energy) into all parts of our being, Physical, Emotional, Mental, and Spiritual.

Finally, learning the LifeBreath Technique will help to resolve old, unhealthy patterns, create positive paradigm shifts, and clear out blockages, allowing you to live more "Chi-fully," filled with light, love, and joy.

WHAT A CONCEPT!!!

The Benefits of Everyday Full Diaphragmatic Breathing & The LifeBreath Technique

Breathing touches every part of our lives. Breath keeps us physically alive, and emotionally and mentally calm and stable. Breath is literally "inspired" and alive in our body, mind, and spirit. The physical, emotional, mental, and spiritual aspects of life are completely interconnected with one another and are dependent upon *"BREATH." These aspects will be fully discussed below.*

<u>P</u>hysically

This section will focus on the physical benefits of full diaphragmatic breathing and the LifeBreath Technique and how we can reduce stress, improve our health, and generate enhanced physical performance.

When we optimize our breathing and create better internal and energetic balance, physiological changes occur. This happens through nervous system balance, increased oxygenation and better breathing coordination. This affects every cell in the body (all of its billions of cells) and also affects the subtle energy systems of the meridians, chakras, and aura.

> *"Nearly every physical problem is accompanied by a disturbance of breathing. But which comes first?"*
> —Hans Weller, MD

> *"Shallow breathers poison themselves."*
> —Paul Bragg

Most of us would agree that our Physical, Emotional, Mental, and Spiritual well-being is interconnected, so intertwined that one can not help but affect the other. Physical ailments can be created from hereditary diseases, drugs (prescription and non-prescription), fatigue, stress, chemical pollution, poison, food additives and preservatives, thought, emotional trauma, accidents, spiritual depravation, germs, viruses ... and the list goes on. All of these things have an effect on the physical body.

We can physically *feel* stress. It's literally in our body – that biting tension on our neck and shoulders or those butterflies in our belly. When we feel emotionally or spiritually empty, we sense it in our physical body too. We have all experienced that heaviness in our heart or that emotional ball in our throat. It's all too interconnected to *not* feel it!

When we breathe normally, we bring in varying qualities and quantities of life energy. When we ***consciously and fully*** breathe, we can alter the quality and quantity of chi and, physically, this can help rid the toxins and stresses that lie in both our body and our energy field. Breathwork assists in detoxifying the body and helps bring in healthy, exciting, new energy. *Breath* resonates aT a very high rate of vibrational energy. Physical mass, our bodies, resonate at a lower rate of vibration. When the high vibration, or supercharged chi, meets the body, the energy level raises up. People can receive a general sense of elation, enthusiasm, and even rapture. Working with your breath, you can physically ***feel*** the vibration of the energy. Radiant health, a general sense of well being, elevated physical performance, and higher energy levels become achievable. Even longevity and growing old gracefully can be attributed to and created by good breathing.

I had done many breathing techniques for over twenty years before I did my first session in full circular breathing. During that first session, I felt more energy than the entire previous twenty years combined. As you may experience, it's quite amazing. Some breathwork is very subtle, others are immediately moving and powerful.

The Chi Kung techniques introduced in my classes and in this book help discover, gather, distribute, balance, and transmit energy through breathing techniques and movement. These are subtle and yet powerful. They will work to enhance all aspects of your life.

The LifeBreath Technique is much less subtle and much more powerful. I call it an "intrusive breath," meaning it does a lot of work in less time. It is "big" and it expedites our positive transformation in life's ever-spiraling evolution.

All human functions are related to breathing Thus, better breathing can help all human functions.

Full conscious breathing techniques have been shown to be effective therapeutically and generate the following improvements:

"Breathing, in short, is the key that unlocks the whole catalog of advanced biological function and development. Is it any wonder that it is so central to every aspect of health? Breathing is the first place, not the last, one should look when fatigue, disease, or other evidence of disordered energy presents itself. Breathing is truly the body's most basic commnication system."
—Sheldon Saul Hendler, MD, Ph.D,
<u>Oxygen Breakthrough</u>

Effects on the Respiratory System

- Enhances energy
- Reduces mental and physical fatigue
- Aids in relief of asthma and other respiratory ailments
- Opens the chest, making breathing easier, and helps energize the Physical, Emotional, Mental, and Spiritual systems
- Helps detoxify and cleanse the lungs
- Better Breathing (halitosis)

> *"One study on treating asthma patients conducted by researchers John Goyeche, Dr. Ago, and Dr. Ikemi suggest that any effective treatment should address suppressed emotions – such as anxiety and self-image, as well as the physical dimension. To achieve this, they encourage correction of poor posture, and helping the person to relax the irrelevent respiratory muscles, while restoring full diaphragmatic breathing ... The good news is that a well-rounded breath work practice will do all these things."*
> —Donna Farhi, The Breathing Book

Effects on the Circulatory System

- Improves blood circulation
- Relieves congestion
- Supplies all major organs with more oxygen, making them healthier
- Increases oxygen in blood supplying muscles and bones with more nutrients

> *"... the relationship between breathing and blood pressure has been known and understood for a long time. It boils down to this: Elevated blood pressure accompanies those bodily states where rapid, shallow breathing prevails. By altering breathing to a slow diaphragmatic mode, blood pressure decreases. Elevated blood pressure is a major American health problem."*
> —Robert Fried, Ph.D., The Breath Connection

Effects on the Lymphatic System

More effective elimination in the lymphatic system

> *"Lymph is a clear fluid containing lymphocytes (T-cells and B-cells of the immune system) which circulate through the channels of the lymphatic system carrying waste away from*

all parts of the body to the lymph nodes. The lymph nodes filter out the wastes in the lymph, particularly bacteria, preventing it from entering the bloodstream, while at the same time allowing the lymphocytes to pass through."
—J. Shields, MD,
<u>Lymph, Lymph Glands and Homeostasis</u>

Jack Shields, MD and lymphologist from Santa Barbara, CA, conducted a study on the effects of breathing on the lymphatic system. Using cameras inside the body, he found that deep, diaphragmatic breathing stimulated the cleansing of the lymph system by creating a vacuum effect which sucked the lymph through the bloodstream. This increased the rate of toxic elmination by as much as 15 times the normal pace.

Effects on the Nervous System

- Calming
- Balancing
- Stimulates and/or calms the nervous system

Effects on the Endocrine System

- Pumps the lymphatic fluid throughout the body, aiding in elimination of toxic wastes
- Strengthens the immune system

Effects on the Urinary System

- Full breathing massages the kidneys
- Full breathing helps move fluid and eliminate it

Effects on the Skin

- Better circulation, healthier, more oxygenated skin
- The skin is the largest organ in the body and needs oxygen
- Improved complexion

Effects on the Digestive System

- Full breathing stimulates and massages the internal organs, making them function better
- Better elimination

Effects on the Energy System and Performance
- Ability to generage internal chi
- Ability to channel energy
- Increases stamina
- Increases coordination
- Positive response to physical needs
- Hastens convalescense
- Improves speech and voice

Used for Pain Management
- Effective for acute and chronic pain managenent
- Relieves aches, pains, and discomfort

Clinical Studies

There are numerous clinical studies and many holistic doctors who support the power and benefits of full diaphragmatic breathing. They concur that Breathwork has positive affects on:

- Heart Disease
- Menopause, hot flashes, PMS, and other female related problems
- Lowering blood pressure
- Ending heart arrhythmia
- Improving long standing patterns of poor digestion
- Increasing blood circulation throughout the body
- Decreasing anxiety and depression (and allowing people to get off addictive anti-anxiety drugs)
- Improving sleep, sleep apnea, and energy cycles
- Decreased addiction, increased recovery
- Reducing stress, fatigue, and anxiety
- Improving and even eliminating asthmatic and respiratory distress
- Pain Relief / Pain Control / Childbirth
- Cancer
- Migraines and headaches
- Infertility
- Smoking and other addictions
- Improving elimination
- Mental concentration and physical performance
- Graceful aging
- Emotional clarity and mastery
- Sexual dysfunction
- Digestive problems
- Sleep apnea and other sleep disorders
- Depression, panic attacks, chronic fatigue, and other associated afflictions

- Improving the immune, lymphatic, circulatory and nervous system
- "Nearly every physical problem"

> *"The simplest and most important technique for protecting your health is breathing. I have seen breath control alone achieve remarkable results: lowering blood pressure, ending heart arthythmias, improving long-standing patterns of poor digestion, increasing blood circulation throughout the body, decreasing anxiety, and allowing people to get off addictve anti-anxiety drugs and improving sleep and energy cycles."*
> —Dr. Andrew Weil, M.D.,
> Clinical Professor of Internal Medicine,
> University of Arizona in Tucson.

Physical :
Insights from Breathwork and Related Life-Lessons

Through my experiences with breathwork, specifically the LifeBreath Technique, and through ongoing life-lessons, I have received powerful insights about caring for my body and soul. Although we are all different, I believe these are universal truths that can help you care for your body as well. And, although breathwork is extremely powerful as a tool for physical well-being, action, and attitude are on the top of the priority list.

Like it or not, you will receive a body that is yours as long as you live. How you take care of it or fail to take care of it can make a tremendous difference in the quality of your life. It is your choice and your lessons to learn.

I suggest the following:

- Breathe! Every physical process involves using oxygen.
- Move your body every day.
- Find exercises that you really enjoy doing.
- Balance your exercise program.
- Cardiovascular, endurance, flexibility, agility, balance, weight bearing, energy work. Remember that even healthy activities can be done out of balance.
- Eat often and eat healthy. If you don't know how to eat healthy, learn.
- Drink lots of water.
- Stay grounded.

> *"If you built castles in the air, your work need not be lost; that is where they should be. Now put the foundation under them."*
> —Henry David Thoreau

- Spend time in nature.

> "To live content with small means; to seek elegance
> rather than luxury, and refinement rather than fashion;
> to be worthy, not respectable, and wealthy, not rich; to study
> hard, think quietly, talk gently, act frankly; to listen to stars
> and birds, to babes and sages, with open heart; to bear all
> cheerfully, do all bravely, await occasions, hurry never. In a
> word, to let the spiritual, unbidden and unconscious, grow up
> through the common. This is to be my symphony."
> —William Henry Channing

My family and me at our camp on Mooselookmeguntic Lake, Maine.

- Get plenty of sleep, rest, and relaxation.
- Meditate daily.
- Create a good work ethic. Do more than is expected of you and do it cheerfully.
- Be very careful how you speak and how you think. There is great power in the spoken word and your thoughts.
- Find a passion in life and follow it.

> "The purpose of life is a life purpose." —Robert Byrne

- Find admirable role models.
- Become a steward. Leave things better than you found them.
- Know that there is a law of reciprocation and karma. Understand that there is a force of action / reaction and the law of choice and

consequences in everything that you think, do, and say.
- Pain and illness can be our greatest teachers.

> *"Of one thing I am certain, the body is not the measure of healing – peace is the measure."* —George Melton

- We project who we are in life.
- Choose who you want to be and project it.
- Attend to the little things in life and do it joyfully
- Sharpen your (life) tools and use them often.
- Be careful not to take on labels or put labels on others.
- Laugh often, *especially at yourself.*
- Play often.
- Learn how to prioritize.
- Learn how to create balance in your life.
- Never stop learning and striving. If you do, it will kill you.
- Find work you really enjoy.

> *"What is it in the end that induces a man to go his own way, and to rise out of unconscious identity with the mass?... It is ... called vocation (which) acts like a law of God ... Anyone with a vocation hears the voice of the inner man; he is called."* —Carl Jung

- Learn about holistic health and eastern and western medicine.
- Take responsibility for your own health.
- Remember the three R's:
- Respect yourself. Respect others. Responsibility in all actions (karma).
- Make happiness a priority. Make your health and well-being a priority. Everyone around you will reap the benefits.
- RELAX !

I received this in one of my first seminars with the Cosmic Breath Institute many years ago. I still use it today as a hand out in many of my seminars.

Stephen James' Totally Subjective Non-Scientific Guide to Illness and Health

How To Get Sick

1. Don't pay attention to your body. Eat plenty of junk food, drink too much, take drugs, have lots of unsafe sex with lot of different partners and, above all, feel guilty about it.
2. Cultivate the experience of your life as meaningless and of little value.
3. Do things you don't like, and avoid doing what you really want. Follow everyone else's opinion and advice, while seeing yourself as miserable and stuck.

4. Be resentful and hyper-critical, especially towards yourself.
5. Fill your mind with dreadful pictures, and then obsess over them. Worry most, if not all the time.
6. Avoid deep, lasting, intimate relationships.
7. Blame other people for all your problems.
8. Do not express your feelings and views openly and honestly. Other people wouldn't appreciate it. If at all possible, do not even know what your feelings are.
9. Shun anything that resembles a sense of humor. Life is a not laughing matter.
10. Avoid making any changes which would bring you greater satisfaction and joy.

How To Get Sicker

1. Think about all the awful things that could happen to you. Dwell upon negative, fearful images.
2. Be depressed, self-pitying, envious, and angry. Blame everyone and everything for your illness.
3. Read articles, books, newspapers, watch TV programs, and listen to people who reinforce the viewpoint that there is NO HOPE. You are powerless to influence your fate.
4. Cut yourself off from other people. Regard yourself as a pariah. Lock yourself up in your room and contemplate death.
5. Hate yourself for having destroyed your life. Blame yourself mercilessly and incessantly.
6. Go to see lots of different doctors. Run from one to another, spend half your time in waiting rooms, get lots of conflicting opinions and lots of experimental drugs, starting one program after another without sticking to any.
7. Quit your job, stop work on any projects, give up all activities that bring you a sense of purpose and fun. See your life as essentially pointless, and at an end.
8. Complain about your symptoms, and if you associate with anyone, do so exclusively with other people who are unhappy and embittered. Reinforce each other's feelings of hopelessness.
9. Don't take care of yourself. What's the use? Try to get other people to do it for you, and then resent them for doing a good job.
10. Think how awful life is, and how you might as well be dead. But make sure you are absolutely terrified of death, just to increase the pain.

<u>P</u>hysical:
LifeBreath Testimonials

"LifeBreath and the skills taught by Beth Bielat have proven to be extremely helpful to both my wife and myself. We have attended her workshops for the past two summers while in Maine. Pain management and the ability to work through it by using LifeBreath Techniques proved invaluable to me during my recovery from recent cardiac surgery. I feel it greatly speeded my recovery process. LifeBreath can have a profound affect on anyone's ability to focus on a healthy lifestyle."
—MH

"Over time, even the grandest of pianos starts to play out of tune, but with delicate adjustments, it can play melodious music once again. If I am the piano then LifeBreath is the tuning instrument that has helped me bring the glorious sound of my soul to light and I am alive and dancing to the energy that now reigns within."
—TW

"As a healthful practice, breathwork seems to revitalize my physical body. It feels right and breathwork, exercise, and meditation seem to compliment each other perfectly. There is a synergistic effect, which is more than addictive." —ZL

<u>Emotionally</u>

This section will focus on how Breathwork improves the emotional well-being of the practitioner specifically through emotional balance, mastery, and control of the Breath and of Self. Reduced stress and tension are attributed to the coping and relaxation skills of conscious Breathing Techniques. Emotional disturbances and behavioral problems, substance abuse and recovery, group dynamics and interpersonal relations are all improved by and interconnected to breathing.

> *"It is certainly not the aim of breathing work, nor is it possible, to have one's breathing unaffected by life or to avoid life's problems. On the contrary, contact with your breathing will make you more open to life's experiences."*
> —Carola H. Spreads

> *"Breath work can help people overcome depression. Many people who are depressed slow way down physically. If we can get them active and getting more oxygen, they often start to talk about their feelings more."*
> —Gay Hendricks, Santa Barbara, Ca.
> Psychologist, leading author and expert on breathwork

We all agree that every human experience, along with the emotion it stirs, is registered in our body and its energy field. We remember it either consciously or subconsciously. It is very interesting that every emotion has a breathing pattern associated with it. When we're depressed we have very stale, shallow, "depressed" breaths. When we are anxious our breaths are sporadic, erratic, and sometimes hysterical. Anger brings forth upper chest, almost hyperventilating type of breathing. Grief and sorrow can make our breath labored, shallow, hard, and painful. Strong emotions often equal intense contraction of breath. This is a short term way of dealing with feelings, but in the long run, the contracted energy robs us of our everyday birth rite of joy, peace, physical energy, and radiant health.

When we experience emotions that are not resolved, not fully experienced and dealt with, we swallow, contract, and stuff the emotions somewhere in our physical memory. Over time, those repressed emotions build up and will continue to until they are resolved. Remember, the aspects of our being, the PEMS systems, are so interconnected that one can not but help affect the other. The LifeBreath Technique is extremely useful to work through emotions as they are happening AND to resolve old "stuck" emotions that are draining our energy and our capacity for being fully alive.

When we repress and don't fully feel, we turn down our energy level temporarily, much like anesthesia, but this does not heal us. We withdraw and stuff the emotion downward. This suppression does NOT equal resolution and healing. These energy patterns touch each part of our being, Physically, Emotionally, Mentally and Spiritually (PEMS). They also become part of our very outlook in life, our paradigm through which we see life. We often become limited in our views in life and the more restricted and heavy we become, the less unrestricted (or loving) energy that we allow in. We meet energy with energy. We are like a full cup that has no more room for anything else. Unless we make room for the positive by ridding ourselves of the things that no longer serve our highest good, we will stay stuck. And unless the pattern in broken and changed, we could go on all of our life blocked, heavy, unhappy, and drained of energy.

Because breath IS, in part, the uncontracted connection, the (loving) energy itself, we can begin to resolve old patterns of restriction through conscious breathing.

Most of us are professional emotional luggage carriers. Somewhere, somehow, people got the idea that it isn't appropriate to express emotions or to fully feel. It isn't OK to cry, grieve, or even laugh too much. So, we created a way of shutting down our emotions. We stuff our emotions deep into the bowels of our being either permanently or for us to work on later. If we don't fully deal with our emotions, at some point we begin running on overload, using our energy inwardly to "hold it all together." Our everyday energy that is intended for joy, health, and love is robbed, stolen away by the lingering unsettled feelings that still wreak havoc with our energy field. Our energy becomes restricted and so do our lives!

Nervous breakdowns, ADHD, sensory overload, depression, and most physical and emotional ailments can be associated with emotional energy that is stuck, blocked, and constricted. All people can make incredible life changes that take old negative patterns and turn the tables to create lives full of radiant health, love, joy, peace, and happiness. *Amazing!*

The LifeBreath Technique has been shown to assist and expedite in the process of integrating those old feelings and allows us to take on a much higher sense of joy. During a Lifebreath session, I often ask a client to set an intention for our time together, to see if we can create a little miracle. People propose things like peace, joy, abundance, clarity, etc. And during (or after) the session they often receive it.

Resolved stress and released past trauma on a conscious or unconscious level (on a cellular level) can be achieved. Old, unhealthy mental tapes and negative programming can be permanently transformed for more peace, creativity, clairity, love, and joy.

When feeling confused, out of sorts, or depressed, look to your breathing.

Notice how your breathing changes as your feelings change. Notice how you can change your breathing and encourage positive changes in your thoughts and emotional state.

<u>E</u>motional:
Insights from Breathwork and Related Life-Lessons

- Breathe! Breath is a key to mastering your emotions.
- True peace, spiritual enlightenment, radiant health, and emotional well-being can not be achieved without forgiveness.
- Forgiveness is the great healer. We must forgive ourselves.

> *"If you must love your neighbor as yourself, it is at least as fair to love yourself as your neighbor."*
> —Sebastein-Roch Nicolas

- By forgiving our past and letting go about worry for our future, we can learn to live joyfully in this moment. Only this moment is real.
- Learn to be present and live in this moment.

> *"Life can be found only in the present moment. The past is gone, the future is not yet here, and if we do not go back to ourselves in the present moment, we cannot be in touch with life."* —Thich Nhat Hanh

- There are different levels of compassion. Work towards compassion without getting caught up in everyone's "stuff."
- No matter who you are, what you have been through, or where you are in life, you absolutely have the power to change your life.
- True happiness comes when we learn that self care begins and ends with ourselves. At that realization, we no longer demand happiness and sustenance from others.

"No one can make you feel inferior without your consent."
　　　　　　　—Eleanor Roosevelt
"Our remedies oft in ourselves do lie."
　　　　　　　—William Shakespeare

"There is no need to run outside for better seeing ... Rather abide at the center of your being; For the more you leave it, the less you learn. Search your heart and see."
　　　　　　　—Lao Tzu in the Tao Te Ching

- Dare to dream!
- No dream is too small or too big.
- Never take away anyone else's dreams.

"There are seasons, in human affairs, when new depths seem to be broken up in the soul, when new wants are unfolded in multitudes, and a new and undefined good is thirsted for. There are periods when to dare is the highest wisdom."
　　　　　　　—William Ellery Channing, 1829

"Insist on yourself; never imitate."
　　　　　　　—Ralph Waldo Emerson

- Make happiness a priority. **Decide** to be happy.
- Live with personal authenticity and integrity.
- Ask, when at odds with yourself or others…
- Would I rather be happy or would I rather be right?
- Remember that life is a journey.
- We can find great reward in loving ourselves.
- Great love and achievements involve great risk

"The worst loneliness is not to be comfortable with yourself."
　　　　　　　— Mark Twain

"I am not afraid of storms, for I am learning how to sail my ship."　　　　　—Louis May Alcott

"In the depth of winter, I finally learned that within me there lay an invincible summer."
　　　　　　　—Albert Camus

"I care not so much what I am to others as what I am to myself."　　　　—Michael Eyquem De Motaigne

"If I have lost confidence in myself, I have the universe against me."　　　　—Ralph Waldo Emerson

"I was brought up to believe that how I saw myself was more important than how others saw me."
—Anwar El-Sadat

"Self-love, my liege, is not so vile a sin as self-neglecting."
—William Shakespeare

"There are seasons, in human affairs, when new depths seem to be broken up in the soul, when new wants are unfolded in multitudes, and a new and undefined good is thirsted for. There are periods when to dare is the highest wisdom."
—William Ellery Channing, 1829

"So much is a man worth as he esteems himself."
—Francois Rabelais, 1532

"What would you attempt to do if you knew you could not fail?" —Dr. Robert Schuller

- There are only two basic human emotions that all other feelings fall under: love and fear. In which state would you like to live your life?
- When you say, "I love you," mean it.
- When you say, "I'm sorry," mean it.
- When you say, "I forgive you," mean it.
- Believe in love at first sight.
- Love deeply and passionately.
- You might get hurt, but it's the only way to live life.
- When you realize you've made a mistake, take immediate steps to correct it.
- One of our deepest fear is not that we are inadequate, it is that we are powerful beyond measure. Overcome your fears and *fly!*
- We all have addictive tendencies. Addiction is being stuck in the past, blocked creative energy, or power turned inwardly on ourselves. Work through your addictions and you will find freedom, joy, and love.

"The courage to be is the courage to accept oneself, in spite of being unacceptable." —Paul Tillich

"It's ok if you mess up. You should give yourself a break."
—Billy Joel

"It is difficult to make a man miserable while he feels worthy of himself and claims kindred to the great God who made him." —Abraham Lincoln.

"Of all afflictions, the worst is self-contempt."
—Berthold Auerbach

> "When you stop drinking, you have to deal with this marvelous personality that started you drinking in the first place."
> —Jimmy Breslin

- People do the best they can.
- Never judge another unless you walk in their shoes.
- Mirroring is the idea that when someone or something bothers you, there is a life lesson to learn.

> "Everything that irritates us about others can lead us to understanding of ourselves." —Carl Jung

> "When we see men of a contrary character, we should turn inwards and examine ourselves." —Confucius

> "Why do you look at the speck of sawdust in your brother's eye and pay no attention to the plank in your own eye? How can you say to your brother, "Let me take the speck out of your eye," when all the time there is a plank in your own eye? You hypocrite, first take the plank out of your own eye, and then you will see clearly to remove the speck from your brother's eye." —MATTHEW 7:3-5

> "If you judge people, you have no time to love them."
> —Mother Teresa

> "Old age is when you realize other people's faults are no worse than yours." —Edgar A. Shoaff

- You are in charge of your emotions.

> "If you do not wish to be prone to anger, do not feed the habit; give it nothing which may tend to its increase. At first, keep quiet and count the days when you were not angry: "I used to be angry every day, then every other day: next, every two then every three days and if you succeed in passing thirty days, sacrifice to the gods in thanksgiving."
> —Epicticus

- Events are just events until the mind comes to judge them.
- Are you a fault-finder or a positive attribute-finder?
- Honor the path that others are on.
- Don't let a little dispute injure a great friendship.
- Love isn't caring FOR others. Love is caring ABOUT others.

> *Dance as if no one were watching.*
> *Sing as if no one were listening*
> *And live as if every day was your last.*
> —Irish proverb

- Transformation occurs when we change our inside world. It does not occur from the world outside us.

    "Love yourself first and everything else falls into line. You really have to love yourself to get anything done in the world."   —Lucille Ball

    "Our remedies oft in ourselves do lie."
        —William Shakespeare

- The past does NOT equal the future.

    "I am not my past. I am walking out of my past."
        —Dr. Phil on Oprah

- Try to make fear a counselor and a motivator.
- KISS ... Keep It Simple Sweety!

The Rules of Being Human *(from Dear Abby)*
(This sums it up pretty gosh darn well for me.)

You will receive a body. You may like it or hate it but it will be yours for as long as you live. How you take care of it or fail to take care of it can make an enormous difference in the quality of your life.

You will learn lessons. You are enrolled in a full-time school called Life. Each day, you will be presented with opportunities to learn what you need to know. The lessons presented are often completely different from those you THINK you need.

There are no mistakes – only lessons. Growth is a process of trial and error and experimentation. You can learn as much from failure as you can from success.

A lesson is repeated until it is learned. A lesson will be presented to you in various forms until you have learned it. When you have learned it (as evidenced by a change in your attitude and behavior), then you can go on to the next lesson.

Learning lessons does not end. There is no stage of life that does not contain lessons. As long as you live, there will something more to learn.

"There" is no better than "here." When your "there" has become a "here" you will obtain another "there" that will again look better than your "here." Don't be fooled by believing that the unattainable is better than what you have.

Others are merely mirrors of you. You cannot love or hate something about another person unless it reflects something you love or hate about yourself. When tempted to criticize others, ask yourself why you feel so strongly.

What you make of your life is up to you. You have all the tools and resources you need. Remember that through desire, goal-setting, and unflagging effort, you can have anything you want. Persistence is the key to success.

The answers lie within you. The solutions to all of life's problems lie within your grasp. All you need to do is ask, look, listen, and trust.

You will forget all this. Unless you consistently stay focused on the goals you have set for yourself, everything you've just read won't mean a thing.

Emotional:
LifeBreath Testimonials

"How (Life) Breath has helped me ...
Allowed me to begin to grieve
Allowed me to feel SAFE enough to grieve
Allowed me to see/feel the NEED to grieve
Allowed me to Realize the Need to have more courage ...
to love and to be loved
Made me aware of my fear.
Made me aware of my need to Trust.
I have more patience and find it easier to accept ...
those small things that in the past seemed irritating.
I feel more Focused and Creative at work ...
better able to relate to and be helpful to colleagues and patients.
I feel I have turned a corner and have begun a journey which may
bring me more love... to allow more love in my life."
—RT

"It has been an amazing tool of transformation for me. Answering questions (helping me to find the answers within myself) and guiding me toward my life purpose of helping others heal. LifeBreath has allowed me to shed years of anger, to find peace within myself, and to become a better mother, wife, daughter, teacher, and friend. Thank you!" —SF

"I was excited on entering and knowing that my life would change, yet I never realized the magnitude of change I would go through and still go through. In training, I was allowed to face my parents, my childself, my shadow, and fears I had buried long ago. There were times I wanted to get up and leave, yet I couldn't, I felt fear but anxious to see more. The connection of self to the group and leader held me in an unconditional feeling of family. In the final week, I was sad yet ready to fly. I knew our family groups would disperse and only by chance would we see each other again. Yet even today I feel the Universal connection to each person I shared this time with. Only in the weeks and months after my training did the full effect influence my life (I guess I felt safe in the group and accepted in ways that I did not experience otherwise). The training became a large part of my life and I notice change constantly. Life is getting easier. I used to fight my way through life, honestly! Now, I am accepting of change and understanding of the Universal forces, which brings happiness, wonderment, and light into my life. Sincere thanks." —GD

Mental

Concentration, clarity, mental performance for physical activities, and a general sense of mental well-being can be attained through breathwork.

Self-Improvement, personal growth and creativity are intertwined within the Breath. Psychic, intuitive, and meditative skills are enhanced through Breathwork and creative expression is also enhanced and accelerated.

> *"With the breath, however, we discover something of great importance. While breathing can well be a completely unconscious process, it also can quite easily become a conscious, intentional practice. That is, while it is critical that respiration, along with most of our bodily processes, be a continuously – and thus unconsciously – driven function, it is also possible to consciously influence and control the flow of breath. This unique quality of the breath – that it can be both conscious and unconscious – makes it a link between the conscious and unconscious aspects of our being."*
> <u>Breathing</u>, Michael Sky, leading expert on breathwork

> *"Love is the experience of taking in the breath of life, without fear. Peace is the results."*
> <u>Until Today</u>, Iyanla Vanzant

> *"Without full awareness of breathing, there can be no development of meditative stability, and understanding."*
> —Thich Nhat Hanh

Breath is voluntary and involuntary, conscious and subconscious, objective and subjective. This is, in part, why it is SO powerful. As a man thinks, so he is. Breathwork can help transform a negative thinker into a positive person with a healthy, creative life.

I call it "monkey mind," two monkeys sitting on either shoulder screaming and *yakking* at you. Many people live with constant chatter in their heads, voices bombarding inner thought, a never-ending stream of self talk. Often, this self talk is negative in its voice and is very difficult to turn off. *Yak, yak, yak, yak.* Breathwork calms the inner voices and opens up the gates for quiet. In the quiet resides intuition, peace, clarity, and self love.

Studies have shown that the "Relaxation Response" is, in part, ignited by relaxed breathing. The brain sends messages to the body that actually slow down many physical functions and the benefits are felt throughout the entire PEMS systems.

One area that breathing has been proven to assist us is in our addictive behavior modification. The addict (we all have some addictive archetypal patterns in us) begins to feel physically more energetic, mentally clear, emotionally open, and spiritually connected as he or she opens their breathing. Through breathwork, a person can feel better on all levels and addiction (and fear) is met with balance (and love).

What would happen if you began to love yourself with love instead of alcohol, sex, drugs, and codependent behavior? Shower yourself with Breath!

<u>M</u>ental:
Insights from Breathwork and Related Life-Lessons

- Breathe...
- Healthy, full, diaphragmatic breathing keeps the mind clear, focused, and relaxed.
- Hang out with positive people.
- Give thanks, then give it again and again. I call this the ***Attitude of Gratitude.***
- Smile when picking up the phone. The caller will hear it in your voice.
- Don't sweat the small stuff. It's mostly small stuff.
- Be impeccable with your words. Speak with integrity.
- Only say things you will sign and date.
- Say only what you mean.
- Become a really good listener.
- Concern yourself with the things that you can influence and let go of those you can't. STOP WORRYING!
- Don't *assume* things.
- Walk the Walk as you Talk the Talk.
- Don't believe gossip.

> *"The mind can actually change physiology."*
> <u>The Relaxation Response,</u> Dr. Benson, MD

- Teach yourself how to think positively.
- You can't afford the luxury of negative thinking.
- ***Gay ga zunta hay ...*** means "NEXT!!!" It's an old Yiddish quote meaning to move on in relationships. Move on in life. Time for a change. Time for new.
- Gay ga zunta hay!
- Don't take anything personally
- Go with the flow and TRUST.

> *"Many a time we've been down to our last piece of fatback. And I'd say, "Should we eat it, or render it down for soap?" Your Uncle Jed would say, "Render it down. God will provide food for us poor folks, but we gotta do our own washin'."*
> —Granny, "The Beverly Hillbillies"

- We are our own Life Script Writer. At the same time, we must hand our lives over to God. What a wonderful duality!

*"Whether you believe you can do a thing or not,
you are right."* —Henry Ford

*'The ideal day never comes. Today is ideal for him who
makes it so."* —Horatio Dresser

*"Nature cannot be tricked or cheated. She will give up to you
the object of your struggles only after you have paid her
price."* —Napoleaon Hill

"I will prepare and some day my chance will come."
—Abraham Lincoln

*"The last of the human freedoms – to choose one's attitude in
any given set of circumstances, to choose one's own way."*
—Viktor Frank

*"The world will freely offer itself to you to be unmasked,
It has no choice, it will roll in ecstasy at your feet."*
—Franz Kafka

"Imagination is more important than knowledge."
—Albert Einstein

*"In the province of the mind, what one believes to be true
either is true or becomes true."* —John Lilly

- When I see an attribute in YOU that I admire, I MUST have it myself, otherwise, I could not recognize it.
- Do you see the cup as half empty or half full? Choose full, and suddenly, you will see that your luck will change.
- Think "win/win." It realy can be achieved.

- **Beware the Six I's**
    I should have
    If only I had
    I judge
    I can't
    I won't
    I am

- Spend a lot of time minding your own business.

- **100th monkey concept:**
    If enough people think the same way, it will effect the whole world. This can be wonderful or it can be dangerous and scary.

The Town Greeter Story

I saw this on a poster in a teacher's restroom at our local high school. I loved it. It goes something like this...

There was a little town in olden times where the Town Greeter met people as they first came into his village.

A family arrived one day and the Town Greeter asked them about their previous home. They said it was a horrible place with war and famine, lots of hatred, and discontented people. The Town Greeter nodded his head and stated that they would find the same here.

Another family arrived a few days later and the Town Greeter also asked them about their previous home. They said it was a wonderful, peaceful place filled with love and beautiful people.

The Town Greeter nodded his head and stated that they would find the same here.

And so it is…

Mental:
LifeBreath Testimonials

"I just want to take this opportunity to thank you for putting together a wonderful personal growth and enlightenment training program. This experience was one of profound personal growth for me. I have learned techniques that help me stay peaceful and centered in my hectic everyday business and personal life. The time I spent was most enjoyable and worthwhile.

I have always been a relatively happy and successful person, but there was always something missing in my life. Your program has helped me to find the missing link. Never before have I found anything quite like the breathwork and training. I have accomplished so much in such a short time. This program empowers you to make positive changes in your life without needing any outside equipment, people, money, or gimmicks! It is so very simple once the light bulb goes on! I hope to share my experiences with all of my friends, family, and co-workers.

The experiences I had during my training have been wonderful and eye opening. I truly am a happier and healthier person. I've developed healthy habits and made new friendships that will be with me for a lifetime." —MO

"Breath is so much a part of my life now. Every day I am finding out new things about myself, and how I can use this to positively interact with people in my daily life. I am looking forward for more experiences through breath." —LR

Spiritual

Psychospiritual transformation, spiritual connection and fulfillment are all a part of LifeBreath and conscious breathing. Through The LifeBreath Technique we connect to our sense of higher purpose, unity consciousness, and inspiration.

*"You are asking me for tools,
and I am giving them to you.
Breathe.
Breathe long and deep,
Breathe in the soft, sweet nothingness of life,
so full of energy,
so full of love.
It is God's love you are breathing.
Breathe deeply and you can feel it.
Breathe very, very deeply and the love will make you cry.
For joy.
For you have met your God,
and your God has introduced you to your soul."*
<u>Conversations with God: An Uncommon Dialogue, Book 3</u>
—Neale Donald Walsch

"Breathing is really the critical link between mind and body, a connection so strong that for thousands of years people all over the world have been using the physical act of breathing to deepen their spiritual lives."
—Susan Davis, "Health and Spirituality Magazine"

"Breath is like a spiritual vitamin. Breathing is the first thing we had to do when we came into this world. It reunites you with all of life, because everything living depends on breathing." —Joyce Mills, Ph.D.

"Ultimately, breathing can be a path to that most essential of human experiences: learning to love. Almost everyone who begins to work with their breathing finds that it is an essential helpmate in their quest to love themselves and others more perfectly. Your breathing will help you feel and clear the barriers to loving yourself, and it will show you where you are holding back in giving and receiving love with others. The spiritual potential of conscious breathing is beautifully expressed in one of the beatitudes of Jesus. Contemporary scholar Neal Douglas Klotz has written a book, "Prayer of the Cosmos," in which he renders the beatitudes in the original Aramaic language spoken by Jesus. The familiar translation says, 'Blessed are the poor

> *in spirit.' But in the original Aramaic language the beatitude had a very different meaning: "Happy and aligned with the One are those who find their home in the breathing."*
> —Gay Hendricks, Conscious Breathing

> *"If you do a relaxed, connected breathing cycle for a few minutes you will experience dynamic energy flows within your body. These energy flows are the merging of spirit and matter."* —Leonard Orr, Rebirthing

Living in black and white is okay. Living in color is magical. Conscious breathing aids people to see in color. It helps us plug into a 220 socket instead of a 110 and live life more fully. We begin appreciating things that never were apparent before. We give thanks each day and learn to unconditionally love on a very different, extraordinary level.

Our inhale is associated with our ability "to receive" (receive the "good stuff" in life ... love, peace, joy, balance, radiant health, and energy). Our exhale is connected with "letting go" and what we do with negativity. When our breath is *just so*, we feel *just right* and very spiritually connected.

Moreover, internal or cellular breathing corresponds to our relationship within ourselves, and external or lung breathing is associated with our environment and our outer world. Thus, our very relationship with our inside world and outside universe are directly affected by our breathing. In other words, how we feel about ourselves and about the world is influenced by how we breathe.

Personally, LifeBreath has changed every part of my life, but the most profound changes have been spiritual. I have come to believe very strongly in attunement, intuition, spiritual connection, and faith.

If we really think about it, the entire universe breathes. It expands and contracts, grows and shrinks, inhales and exhales. Being in tune with our breath automatically makes us feel that we are *one* with the universe and with nature.

Spiritual:
Insights from Breathwork and Related Life-Lessons

- *Breathe...*
  for within The Breath you draw in is spirit and all the "good things" of life.
- Remember that every day is a gift.
- Remember that your loved ones are just temporarily on loan to you.
- They may be recalled at any given moment.
- Every relationship is holy, from the stranger at the grocery store to your beloved ones.
- Show people your "heart smile" everywhere you go. You'll be surprised how it is received. Become a beacon of light wherever you walk.
- Communicate with God, nature, goddess, universal chi…whatever you call it.

> *"I maintain that cosmic religious feelings is the strongest and noblest incitement to scientific research."* —Albert Einstein

- Learn about unconditional love.

  > *"Each time we drop our masks and meet heart to heart ... Each time we are able to remain open to suffering, despite our fear and defensiveness, we sense a love in us which becomes increasingly unconditional… Awakening from our sense of separateness is what we are called to do in all things."* —Ram Dass

  > *"The purse of the heart is identical in all – place therein the treasure."* —Agni Yoga teachings

- Believe in miracles.
- Learn to recognize small coincidences and happen-stance as a strong force in helping you see and hear spiritual guidance.
- Learn about attunement.
- Having patience is having faith in the Divine.
- We are never healed... we are made whole. This can only occur from within.
- Listen to your intuition. Strive to be intuitive.

  > *"What the inner voice says*
  > *Will not disappoint*
  > *The hoping soul."*
  >   —Schiller 1797

- Meditate

  > *"We need to find God, and he cannot be found in noise and restlessness. God is the friend of silence."* —Mother Teresa

- Trusting in God and Breath

  > *Not, what I am, O Lord, but what Thou Art;*
  >   *That, that alone can by my soul's true rest;*
  > *Thy love, not mine, bids fear and doubt depart,*
  >   *And stills the tumult of my troubled breast.*
  >
  > *Girt with the love of God, on every side,*
  >   ***I breathe that love as heaven's own healing air;***
  > *I work and pray, and follow still my guide,*
  >   *And fear no foe, escaping every snare.*
  >
  > *'Tis what I know of Thee, my Lord and God,*
  >   *That fills my soul with peace, my lips with song;*
  > *Thou art my health, my joy, staff, my rod;*
  >   *I lean on Thee, in weakness I am strong.*
  >   —*Psalm 195* Hobatius Bonar

- Know that the Lord works from the inside out.

 > *"The world works from the outside in. The world would take people out of the slums. Christ takes the slums out of people, and then they take themselves out of the slums. The world would mold men by changing their environment. Christ changes men, who then change their environment. The world would shape human behavior, but Christ can change human nature."* —Ezra Taft Benson

 > *"Often people attempt to live their lives backwards; they try to have more things, or more money in order to do more of what they want, so they will be happier. The way it actually works is the reverse. You must first be who you really are, then do what you need to do, in order to have what you want."* —Margaret Young

Have you ever heard the story of the Golden Buddha?

Once upon a time, some geologists were exploring an area in the Far East. During their excavation they came upon an immense clay Buddha. One evening, it began to rain. The workers covered the statue as best they could with the supplies they had at hand. However, during the night their tarps leaked and the Buddha got wet. The next morning, to everyone's surprise, there were some points on the Buddha that were sparkling through the mud. After careful hammering and chiseling, an incredible Golden Buddha appeared. You see, many centuries before, this area was a monastery and it had been attacked and the monks, fearing loss of life and a stolen irreplaceable work of art, covered the Buddha with clay. The Golden Buddha had been hidden for years behind a mask of mud.

And this is how we may perceive the Golden Buddha that resides in each of us. Lather ourselves with mud and clay, try to hide our golden essence as we may, but there is still a golden Buddha that resides in each of us. The fact that the monks had to hide the Buddha can be likened to our own feelings of exposure and hiding our golden essence. The rain shows that it can glisten through when we least expect it. Our work in life is like the hammer and chisel, whittling away our hard exterior. The awe that the workers must have felt when they saw that golden Buddha is like the awe we feel when we lift the vales of fear and show to the world our hearts.

Spiritual:
LifeBreath Testimonials

"There is a place that exists in my world now that I never knew before I started LifeBreath. It is a place where I have met my true self and not the person that others had helped me define. In opening up my heart I have seen with new eyes, a world that is mine and mine alone and I am at peace there."
—TW

"Breathwork has helped me to get more in contact with my emotions. Combined with a positive mental and spiritual outlook, breathwork has brought me more in contact with the spirit world. I can feel the Spirit connection moving through me in the form of Energy. I find myself becoming overwhelmed by the Energy of Love, coming to me through the entire Universe. It becomes an emotional opening taking on the form of tears of Joy." —ZL

Chakra Basics

Our bodies have an amazing system of energy center called chakras. They are located both in the body and around the body. The human chakra system is the bridge between the body and soul and it is a structure to help us organize our experiences. One of the simplest ways I have come to understand chakras is like a filing cabinet where we store our experiences and memories. Most people are actually very aware of their chakras, they just never connected these feelings to a system. Here are some examples:

- *Have you ever had a broken heart? You can actually FEEL the heaviness in your heart. You can feel it in your heart chakra.*

- *Have you ever been very nervous? You can FEEL it in your belly; butterflies, nausea, nervousness. These feelings are your chakras talking to you.*

- *If you've ever been sexually stimulated, you have felt your first and second chakras.*

- *How about that ball in your throat when you feel an emotion coming up? There's actually a physical ball! We don't feel this in our big toe, it's in our throat!*

- *We all FEEL our chakras.*

The Seven Major Chakras

Wheels of Light

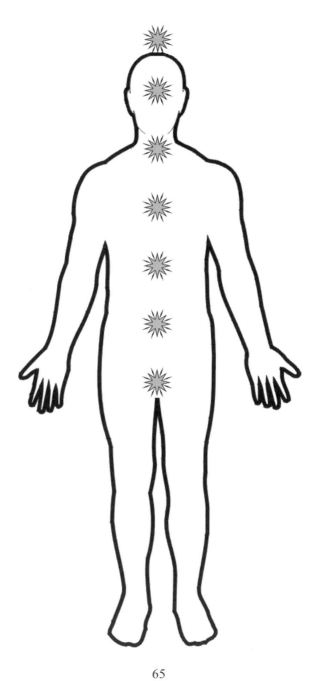

Ancient artifacts from all over the world have been found illustrating the human chakra system. The Chinese, Greek, Egyptian, Roman and Native American cultures all knew of this energy. Much of our knowledge was lost during the Dark Ages when science and spiritual matters separated, but new proof and old history has brought the Chakra system back into the limelight.

Each place where a bone touches bone or there is a nerve center, there is a chakra. We have about 122 secondary chakras throughout the body and seven major chakras along the spinal access. Each major chakra has a color, size, and shape, rotation and spin, intensity or *openess* (amount of energy actually being produced) and a nerve plexus and gland associated with it. Each also has a physical, emotional, creative, and celestial component and each has its own purpose and viewpoint based on the area of consciousness that it influences. Each person lives more dominantly in connection with a particular chakra's influence.

The health of a chakra can be determined by its rotation, radiance, spin, and diameter. This is also associated with the health of the whole person.

Climbing the Chakra Ladder

As we grow in consciousness, we move through the chakra system from lower to higher, naturally. We begin our life experience in the material world and learn about survival through our parents, family, and community. We then move into our own personal experience through our own eyes and our own relationships. We then move on to learn about our own self image and how we relate to our external world. Although all the chakras are interconnected, these are all considered mainly first, second, and third chakra living.

As we move toward the fourth chakira, we grow from being fear based to being more love based beings. The fourth chakra is where we begin living in our higher aspects of life in connection with love, compassion, and spirit. The three upper chakra ignite intuition, creativity, and spiritual connection.

The primary aspects of each chakra are listed below and will be reviewed in more detail later in this section.

Chakra VII	Spirituality, divine purpose, destiny, spiritual seeking, fusion of the body and spirit
Chakra VI	Mind, intuition, insight, wisdom, inner vision, world service, meditative practices
Chakra V	Higher Will, self expression, communication, nurturing
Chakra IV	Love, compassion, forgiveness, life harmony, soul issues
Chakra III	Ego, personality, self esteem, self image, fear, judgment, mental, intellectual, personal power
Chakra II	Sexuality, physical desire, work, emotional, relational
Chakra I	Material world, security, safety, survival, grounding

As well as being individually focused on various aspects of living, the chakras are also seperated into three major groups. These groups symbolize the develpement of human beings from lower to higher consciousness.

Chakra V, VI, VII   Upper / God's World / Spiritual

Chakra IV   Middle / Transition between the two worlds

Chakra I, II, III   Lower / Mankind / Physiological

Chakras Relating to Breath

Since the chakras act as a filing cabinet or storage house where our Physical, Emotional, Mental, and Spiritual (PEMS) aspects of self come together, it relates directly to breathing. The relationships of how, where, and when the breath enters the body, along with the quality, quantity, and the intention of our breath directly affects the chakra and, thus, the quality and our perception of life. Every part of our health is directly affected by our breathing.

Before we can make changes in our lives, we must make fully conscious our unwanted patterns. We climb the chakras to build the self. Chakras are the gateway through which the soul enters our physical bodies and our lives. Chi is the source of energy. **Breathing is our most prevalent, abundant source of chi.**

We work with our Emotions –

E-motion = movement of energy and spirit.

The chakras are specialized energy centers and they connect us to multi-dimensional universes of energy. Each center correlates to a different nerve plexus, physiological system and endocrine system. The endocrine glands are part of the master control system that affects the physical body through the chakras. This is especially useful when working multidimensionally with any kind of illness. We can look at the illness and better understand what chakra is being affected, as well as all the Physical, Emotional, Mental and Spiritual (PEMS) aspects connected to that center.

Neurophysiological and Endocrine Associations of the Chakras

Chakra	Nerve Plexus	Physiological System	Endocrine System
I	Sacral-Coccygeal	Reproductive	Gonads
II	Sacral	Genitourinary	Leydig
III	Solar	Digestive	Adrenals
IV	Heart	Circulatory	Thymus
V	Cervical Ganglia Medulla	Respiratory	Thyroid
VI	Hypothalamus Pituitary	Autonomic Nervous System	Pituitary
VII	Cerebral Cortex Pineal	CNS Central Control	Pineal

—Taken from *Vibrational Medicine,* Dr. Richard Gerber, MD.

As you read about each center, consciously breathe into that area. Draw your breath there to help feel the energy.

Chakra Basics

Chakra I

1st Chakra

Focus: Life Force
  Physical / instinctual / survival / tribal

Location: Base of the spine

Color: Red

Physiological: Physical Body Support, Bones, Joints, Spine, Blood, Immune System

Possible Associated Abnormalities: Colon, Rectum, Sphincter Diseases

Sacred Truth: *"All is one"*

First Chakra energy:

Security	Safety	Groundedness
Balance	Survival	Loyalty
Justice	Honor	Family Values
Tribal Values	Family Power	Tribal Power

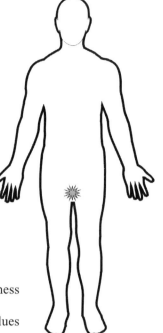

Reminder: Breathe into your lower belly as you read this section to focus your energy on the first chakra.

The first chakra is where we hold our grounding, group belief patterns such as loyalty, honor, and justice and is also the foundation of physical, emotional, and mental health. When the first chakra is balanced we feel well-grounded, connected to our world, balanced, safe, and filled with authenticity and integrity. When a person has a strong balanced first chakra, he or she is usually earth friendly, has a healthy urge to live, is practical and knows how to take care of his/her self. That person has a strong sense of family identity (biological and/or spiritual) and bonding.

When the first chakra is unbalanced or closed, people often feel blocked, frustrated, negative, and separate, may feel overwhelmed by this separatism, and may have the urge to control others. Often they feel they must always be "right." When the first two chakras are dysfunctioning, it may be associated to outdated mental tapes and holding on to the past. Too much energy in the first center leads to paranoia and too little manifests in a "no will to live" attitude. There is often difficulty manifesting in the physical world and there may be a complete forgetting of the soul. It is here where we can get overwhelmed with fear for physical survival and fear of abandonment. Excluding others, prejudice and illusions of superiority are shadows of this center. The first chakra is the seedbed of many destructive patterns.

First Chakra Destructive Patterns:

Negativism
"Everything is wrong. Everything is done TO me. The world is a horrible scary place. Let me see if I can tell you everything that is wrong with you and wrong with me. Poor, poor, pitiful me and you."

Me Against You
"Everyone is out to get me. People in this world are out to get each other. I'm gonna screw you before you can screw me."

Caveman Syndrome
"Me Tarzan, You Jane. I take care of you" (oh, and abuse you, too).

Peter Pan Syndrome
"I'll never grow up. I don't want to grow up."

Seeing RED
Lots and lots of anger.

Mother Hen Syndrome
"I'll take care of everyone" (except me, of course).

Codependency - Helplessness
"I want someone else to take care of me."

Baby Doll Syndrome
"I'll stay helpless and cute so everyone takes care of me and feels sorry for me."

Drugs, Sex, and Rock and Roll
"I'll avoid my problems by using drugs and alcohol, using people, and never getting quiet with myself."

Bad Partners
"I'll seek out people who live out the empty patterns of victimization and abuse that I know so well."

Other patterns:
Many mental illnesses and physical dependencies can be easily linked to first chakra imbalances like dysfunctional families, alcoholism, drug abuse, overeating, and obsessive compulsive disorder, multiple personalities, and depression.

How to Begin Balancing the First Chakra

Begin the shift by breathing into the abdomen and lower back. Spend time each day emphasizing low belly breathing in a quiet and safe space. Try to make belly breathing a habit.

Second, work on the shift from the mind/body to spiritual. Daily practice of exercise like tai chi/ chi kung or yoga will ground the body and make it healthy and strong.

Next, practice LifeBreath style breathing to help transform old negative patterns and integrate new healthy patterns of thinking about the past, present, and future. This will help release the past, let you stop worrying about the future, and live more joyfully in each moment.

Lastly, continuously work on creating new ways of thinking and paradigm shifts that positively influence your life. For example, if you have struggled with alcoholism, find an AA group or someone who can help you. If you have previously been attracted to people who bring you down, find new friends with fun interests that you have in common. Read books, join groups, spend time in meditation and reflection. Decide just how you would like to change your life and DO IT! Just do it!!

Questions to Ask Yourself to Understand and Transform Your First Chakra

- What beliefs do I have that I inherited from my family and/or growing up that no longer serves my highest good?
- Do I feel safe in this world? Are there situations where I feel helpless and/or fearful?
- What is my personal code of ethics? Write your code of ethics down and follow them. Include your ideas about honor, justice, and loyalty *and make NO exceptions.*
- Do I have a good ability to discern as to when to trust and when to question?

Affirmations are positive statements about the truths you are actively creating. Using affirmations is a powerful way of changing your self talk and thus becoming more active in the creation of change in your life. Read them aloud at least twice daily.

Affirmations for the First Chakra

- My 1st chakra is open and balanced.
- I am cared for, I am loved.
- I feel at home with myself.
- I feel firmly planted.
- I am safe in my physical body.

Chakra II

2nd Chakra

Focus: Relationships
    Sexuality/worthiness/creative urges/self image

Location: Sexual/Sacral
Color: Orange

Physiology: Uterus, Ovaries, Cervix, Vagina, Prostate, Testes, Bladder, Large Intestine, Rectal Area

Possible Associated Abnormalities: Cervical and Uterine Cancer, Colitus, Irritable Bowel Syndrome, Bladder Tumors, Sexual Dysfunction, Lower Back Pain

Sacred Truth: *"Honor one another"*

Second Chakra Energy:

Control	Boundaries	Survival Instincts
Relationships	Financial Energy	Work Ethics
Personal Power	Creativity	Risk Taking
Authority		

Reminder: Breathe into your belly as you read this section to focus your energy to the second chakra.

Our second energy center is all about partnerships and relationships that satisfy our physical needs. It isn't only about our sexuality, it is also about our ability to learn to explore the power of choice and how we experience and control our external lives. Things like money, finances, work, taking risks, and being resilient are all second chakra oriented. It is here where we hold our self sufficiency and survival instincts, including the fight or flight response. A shadow trait of the second chakra is disempowering or using others for our own advantage. From a spiritual perspective, we learn here that all relationships are spiritually oriented, including our relationships with money, strangers, the world, and even our comfort with risk taking.

When the second chakra is balanced, we feel safe and spiritually guided. Risks are actually exciting and fun. We have the ability and stamina to survive financially and physically. Our instincts are good. We are passionate, creative, charming, ethical, alert, and sexually comfortable. We are filled with goodness (God-ness). We are passionate about merging our life with others, filled with enthusiasm and desire for intimacy. We are comfortable with materialism, authority, control, and ownership.

Physically, we are resilient, healthy, and filled with physical strength. Our alert system works well and we feel balanced. We are sexually magnetic and comfortable with sensuality of all kinds. Mentally and emotionally calm and peaceful, a second chakra balanced person "knows" to act through his or her heart and knows we are "in the world, but not of it." We get a true sense of a good, positive personal identity. We feel powerful about choices, relationships, creative energy, sexual energy, money, ethics, and personal power.

Unbalanced, we believe we *are* our feelings and our intense urges. Fear of loss of control, being controlled by others, and physical fears are prominent. Risk taking is scary and trust is very hard to come by. Betrayal, fear of financial loss, addiction, abandonment, and impotence are all unbalanced second chakra traits. Being overly sensitive to criticism or having a deep sense of unworthiness can be felt here. Addiction to power and delusions of grandeur are common as well.

Physically, being in our body may be uncomfortable. Sexuality may be unbalanced and difficult at either end of the spectrum. We can either be sexually overactive to try to cope with our feelings of control or inactive/impotent due to fear. Life will seem scary. Jealousy, possessiveness, hatred, aggression, obsession, addiction, and rage are also second chakra characteristics.

Destructive Patterns:

- Don Juan Syndrome: "Looking for love in all the wrong places."
- "I can't take any risks, I'll get hurt."
- "I'm never safe."
- "I'm so ashamed."
- "I'll control everyone and everything in order to feel safe."
- "I need to be needed by others."
- "I follow all my physical urges."
- "Creatively, I'm a mess."
- "I'm better than you."
- "I control you."
- "Sex is scary."
- "Sex is how I control you."
- "I feel frantic, jealous and full of rage."
- "I'd do anything to have you."

How to Begin Balancing the Second Chakra

Continue to BREATHE into your belly and solar plexus. The breath will bring energy and intuition into your second energy center. Practicing the LifeBreath Technique will expedite healing the feelings of distrust, unworthiness, and control. Bringing in that Breath of Life will enhance the feelings of trust, connection, and intuition.

Meditate on **trust** while breathing deeply and gently into your tan tien or hara (second center) throughout the day. Become a habitual belly breather so that you can consistently bring new life and energy into your consciousness. Take action to learn to trust. Begin to meditate on the "big picture" in life. Start by taking small actions that, although out of your safety box, you can DO. Learn that ALL relationships are holy and spirit is always in your corner. Small things like smiling at someone at the grocery store, taking a different route to work that is a little adventuresome, or trying something new that you always wanted to do are all actions headed in the right direction.

Know that everything is a lesson and there really aren't any wrong choices, just more or less appropriate, and you will survive and grow stronger with each new decision and learn to trust.

Questions to Ask Yourself to Understand and Transform Your Second Chakra

- Do my fears have authority over me? Fear of loss of control? Fear of loss of money? Fear of comfort? Fear of new things?
- Do I allow my creative juices to flow? Do I act upon my ideas? Do I go after what I want actively or passively?
- What goals do I have and do I act upon them?
- Am I a controlling person? Control of others, circumstances, finances, sexuality, etc.?
- Or do I allow others to control me?
- Do I negotiate my ethics according to my situation?
- Do I have the capacity to "trust?"

Affirmations for the Second Chakra

- I am always safe.
- I honor myself and others.
- My 2nd chakra is open & balanced.
- It is safe for me to feel pleasure.
- I feel at home in my body.
- I trust myself and my instincts.

Chakra III

3rd Chakra

Focus: Power
    Self-esteem/self-identity/personal power/anger

Location: Solar Plexus

Color: Yellow

Physiology: Abdomen, Middle Digestive
    Tract, Liver, Gallbladder, Kidneys,
    Spleen, Middle Spine

Possible Associated Abnormalities:
    Digestive Organ Diseases,
    Ulcers of the Stomach or Duodenum,
    Diabetes

Sacred truth: *"Honor oneself"*

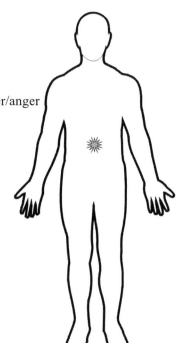

Third Chakra Energy:

Personal Power	Self-Esteem	Self-Responsibility
Self-Respect	Self-Discipline	Ambition
Courage	Generosity	Ethics

Reminder: Breathe into your solar plexus as you read this section to focus your energy to the third chakra.

    The third chakra relates to our perception of ourselves to the outside word through either a healthy or less healthy view of personal power and self esteem. In this center we move away from group thought and closer to understanding ourselves. Here we mature in our understanding in our relationships to ourselves and the outside world and how we take care of ourselves through self-respect. We become separate from our "tribe" and identify our own way of thinking, our own strengths, and our ability to be whole, but separate.

    Balanced in the third center, we feel comfortable with ourselves, generous, and have strength in character and commitment. We are good decision-makers and feel safe taking risks. We have good judgement, but are not judgmental. We have a solid sense of identity and are personally mature with balanced values and ethics. We are orderly, realistic, gratified, and like to make things happen. There is an inner beauty and a shift from ego dominance to soul dominance with an innate recognition of truth, goodness, and beauty. Although we have realistic future goals that we take action on, we also like to dream, be creative, and test "the rules."

This balanced person recognizes that the way to heal is not *out,* but *through* and takes action throughout their life to continue to grow and heal. They realize that there is self-responsibility in taking a course of action towards higher consciousness and their intense ego becomes the joy of the their soul.

Unbalanced, the third center is riddled with fear; fear of rejection, criticism, failure, physical appearance, and loss. We have an unrealistic belief system about the truth that spawns shame, victim consciousness, jealousy, inadequacy, greed, struggle, unhealthy need for respect and love, separateness and fragmentation. The challenges of the third chakra are constantly helping us re-evaluate our sense of power and self in relationship to the outside world. Sometimes, we become fake, materialistic, and overly success oriented with an overwhelming sense to merge and become one of the crowd. We believe life is happening to and outside us and become forgetful of our soul. We get caught up in our physical appearance, professional status and our material "stuff" and forget about prayer, love, intuition, and spirit.

Destructive Patterns:

- "I hate how I look."
- "I never feel good enough."
- "The car I drive, the house I live in and the job I have is what's most important."
- "Money, money, money, power, power, power, greed, greed, greed."
- "I don't go out unless my hair and nails are perfect."
- "I am afraid."
- "I judge you."
- "I give up."

How to Begin to Balance the Third Chakra

The third chakra is located around the solar plexus. This is also an area where we hold a lot of tension and contracted breath. For many, it is a difficult place to breathe into, so focusing the breath and your attention here will be of great value. I have found it helpful to roll the breath from low belly into my diaphragm and rub my diaphragm in a gentle, circular manner. This brings my body/mind attention to the area and relaxes and soothes the muscles. Rubbing and/or tapping can be used on any of the chakras.

The LifeBreath Technique can be used to resolve energy around personal power, fear, and judgement. When we learn or realize self-esteem and self-respect and truly begin to LOVE ourselves, we can forgive our past, because that past created who we are today *(and that's a good thing because we like who we have become)!*

Become a habitual belly to heart breather by filling both belly and chest with air. Your natural breath will become circular, gentle, full, and relaxed.

Meditate on your inner beauty.

Take time each day for being grateful. Remember that your body (hair, nails, makeup, clothes, etc.) and your "stuff" (car, house, and belongings) are outside you and just a small piece of the puzzle of what is important.

Find your passion and take steps to follow it.

Questions to Ask Yourself to Understand and Transform the Third Chakra

- Do I like myself?
- Do I respect myself?
- Do I need approval of others?
- Do I feel competent?
- What and who am I afraid of?
- Am I judgmental (to others, to myself)?
- Am I overly concerned about my appearance?
- Do I follow my dreams and passions or do I more often feel a victim of circumstance?

Affirmations for the Third Chakra

- I am perfect and whole just as I am.
- I like myself.
- I respect myself.
- I am following my passion.
- I am not to judge. I am open.
- My 3rd chakra is open & balanced.
- I create a positive environment for myself every day.
- I am impeccably honest with myself and others.

Chakra IV

4th Chakra

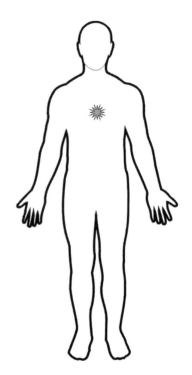

Focus: Balance
   Giving & receiving love/life
   harmony/soul issues

Location: Heart

Color: Green

Physiology: Heart, Blood Vessels,
   Lungs, Breasts

Possible Associated Abnormalities:
   Immune Disease, Heart Disease,
   Thymus Disease

Sacred Truth: *"Love is divine power"*

Fourth Chakra Energy:

Love	Forgiveness	Compassion
Inspiration	Trust	Healing
Dedication	Hope	

Reminder: Breathe into your heart as you read this section to help focus your energy to your fourth chakra.

Our fourth chakra, centered at the heart, is the meeting place of our Higher and Lower self, and is a place of healing and extreme importance. In our heart we make the shift from unconscious to conscious living. It is here where we open the gateways to our fifth, sixth, and seventh chakras and higher consciousness. We meet longing and pain with spiritual meaning and purpose behind our suffering.

Balanced in the fourth chakra, we feel both loved and loving in a human and spiritual sense. We learn to respect ourselves and others through compassion and forgiveness. It is in this center where we hold warmth, understanding, and nurturing. We are expressive, playful, and lighthearted and carry an inner joy for loving and living when the heart center is open. We project a sense of harmony and inner beauty. Working on fourth chakra issues, we learn that it is through compassion and forgiveness that we can heal ourselves and that any past experience can be viewed through the eye of spirit to guide us toward more love and more beautiful living.

When our heart center is out of balance, repressed emotions can harbor many different levels of hatred, pain, bitterness, jealousy, co-dependency, and possessiveness. These emotions can be directed toward others, but they can also be directed toward ourselves. Because this is our love and compassion center, when it is not balanced we feel "UN"... un-balanced, un-inspired, un-compassionate, un-expressive, un-nurtured and even un-loved and un-loving.

The expression "cold hearted" probably came from the energy read out of someone with a closed heart. This life scenario can be very painful, not only living with the pain from the past, but also living with fear of pain in the present and future. Until the heart center begins to open more fully, forgiveness for self and for others may feel difficult or virtually impossible. We must first open our third chakra (intellect) before we can be fully in our hearts. The mind is paradoxically the gateway to the heart. True positive thinking is a mental stance of surrender, simply trusting the process. According to the ancient art of spiritual alchemy, the marriage of Mind and Heart is the sacred marriage of our masculine and feminine natures. Once this union is achieved, we become whole and no longer seek the balance outside ourselves in co-dependent ways.

Destructive Patterns:

- "I'll never forgive myself."
- "I'll never forgive him/her."
- "I've been hurt so many times, I can never love again."
- "I hate you."
- "I hate myself."
- "I'll love you, but only with these conditions."
- "I'm stuck in the material world. I don't have time for the love stuff."

How to Begin Balancing the Fourth Chakra

Because this is our love/compassion center, breathing into the heart region automatically brings us to a place of more loving energy. Breath IS love energy. It's the energy that connects us to life, nature, and even God. So, focused attention and intention in the heart carries vibrant, peaceful harmony from above and below. There are three chakras below and three chakras above. This makes the heart the center of our being. When you breathe into the heart, feel your lungs expand from bottom to top. Allow them to expand down, up, front, and back. Fill your entire heart center from the solar plexus to the throat. Become a habitual full heart breather.

A LifeBreath session can make profound changes in the way that we view our lives. I have seen people shift from being unforgiving, hateful, and closed to being open, forgiving, and loving. Releasing the past and being able to see our past in a positive, spiritual way is a very common paradigm shift that we see students of LifeBreath experience. There can be a general shift to having more trust about the future, which is a major hurdle in living life more fully. The Lifebreath Technique helps integrate our past and future and teaches us how to live more profoundly and beautifully in the present moment.

Focusing on a more loving way to live will assist us in opening our hearts on a day to day basis. Basically, our intentions, or our paradigms in life, can be categorized into two views – either coming from a place of **love** or **fear**. When I am faced with any decision, any thought or any attitude, I ask myself which place I am coming from, love or fear. I know that when my heart is open and I am connected to my higher self, love comes through. I also know that when I have negative or unloving thoughts, I am coming from a place of fear (and all the sub-headings of fear; negativity, greed, hatred, prejudice, etc.). Begin to focus on your heart, and the love and compassion that will manifest will amaze you. It is only through forgiveness, love, and learning to open our hearts that we can truly find happiness and peace.

Questions to Ask Yourself to Understand and Transform Your Fourth Chakra

- What emotions and memories do I still need to heal?
- Who do I need to forgive?
- Do I carry anger, rage and bitterness?
- Am I often anxious or depressed?
- Do I understand forgiveness?
- Do I have healthy relationships?
- Do the memories of my past stop me from having intimate relationships with others or even myself?
- Do I view the world and people as generally positive, wonderful, and fun or generally negative, scary and a lot of work?

Affirmations for the Fourth Chakra

- The past does NOT equal the future.
- I am loved.
- I am loving.
- I am safe.
- I chose love over fear.
- My Heart is open & balanced.
- I am abundantly loved.
- I trust.
- I freely forgive myself and others.

Chakra V

Fifth Chakra

Focus: Will
   Creative Expression/Communication/Higher Will

Location: Throat

Color: Blue

Physiology: Neck, Thyroid, Teeth, and Gums

Possible Associated Abnormalities:
   Laryngitus, Thyroiditus,
   Diseases associated to the Thyroid,
   Larynx, Teeth, and Gums

Sacred Truth:
   "I surrender Divine Will to my personal will"

Fifth Chakra Energy:

Higher will	Personal knowledge
Personal-authority	Surrender
Choice and Consequences (Karma)	Faith

Reminder: Breathe into your throat as you read this section to focus your energy on the fifth chakra.

The fifth chakra is all about choice, will, surrender, and consequences. In essence, it's about personal power, but in a different sort of way. It is here where we begin to understand the "bigger picture." There are times in our lives when we actually think we are in charge. Soon we find out that "even the best laid plans of mice and men often go astray" and that God or nature or spirit or whatever **you** call it, is actually more in charge than we may know. Choice after choice, time after time, we will either get stuck or we will experience a change (i.e. LifeBreath) and we can eventually turn our lives over to intuition and listening to our higher guidance.

When centered in the fifth chakra we are truthful, creative, and expressive and we have a strong, connected, and balanced will. We sense our spiritual connection, get guidance from our intuition, and recognize the difference between fearful thoughts and higher consciousness. We realize that our thoughts co-create our destiny and that life is filled with choices and consequences that continually guide us toward our higher purpose. We beat our own drum and we are constantly moving toward our unique life's work.

When the fifth energy center is shut down, there is no belief in higher will or higher purpose. Life is just a mundane, day to day grind with little or no purpose. We feel unexpressive, uncreative, unimaginative, uninsightful, and uninspired. We see no consequences for our right or wrong actions. Usually, our self-esteem is low and we are very judgmental and even prejudiced. It's easy to be dishonest because of our misconception about choices and it may be very difficult to keep our word.

How to Begin Balancing the Fifth Chakra

Begin with practices that promote self expression and begin following your heart. Figure out whether you feel as though you have been squelched expressively and energetically. Then take action by following new paths of assertion and voice. Meditate and breathe in your higher will. Listen to your dreams and aspirations. Find ways to nurture your creative juices. Work on connecting your lower and higher will. Keep the promises you make to others and to yourself. If this has been a problem in the past or if you seem to not fulfill your commitments and goals, find new ways to hold yourself accountable.

Do a LifeBreath session and feel free to express! People often express themselves loudly. The physical feelings can be very intense in the throat, but after a session a new voice is found and higher will expressed. When energy is released in the fifth chakra, amazing things happen during a LifeBreath session.

During one of my own sessions I remember toning (making sound) instinctually. After my session my voice changed and my ability to express myself also changed. I would have never been able to talk about love, light, connection, and intimate spiritual feelings had I not experienced that session and the release of my throat energy.

Questions to Ask Yourself to Understand and Transform Your Fifth Chakra

- Is it easy or hard for me to express myself?
- Who/what brings up my issues around expression?
- Do I listen to higher guidance/intuition?
- Do I seek to control others?
- Do I allow others to control me?
- Am I judgmental?
- Do I have strong willpower?
- What bargains do I make with myself when my willpower is low?

Affirmations for the Fifth Chakra

- My 5th chakra is open & balanced.
- I communicate clearly and easily.
- I trust my creative intuition.
- I follow the path of my highest good.
- I receive intuition.
- I act upon my intuition.
- I let go of judgment.
- My willpower is strong and graceful.

Chakra VI

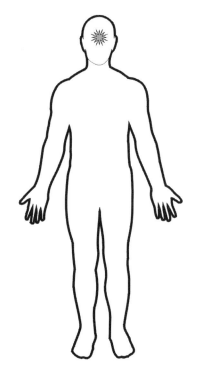

6th Chakra

Focus: Vision

Inner vision/Service to the world
    Spirituality/Compassion

Location: Third eye

Color: Indigo

Physiology: Brains, Eyes, Ears, Nose

Possible Associated Abnormalities:
    Sinus Problems, Cateracts,
    Endocrine Imbalances.
    All Types of Cerebral Dysfunction.

Sacred Truth: *"Seek only the Truth"*

Sixth Chakra Energy:

Intelligence	Mental Body	Psychological Skills
Wisdom	Reasoning	Evaluation Skills
Intuitive Insight	Understanding	

Reminder: Breathe into your third eye (brow) as you read this section in order to focus your energy to the sixth chakra.

The sixth chakra activates our life lessons that lead to higher wisdom, understanding, and clairvoyance ("clear vision"). Truth and illusion are sorted out through active evaluation, receiving inspiration, insights, and intuitive messages.

When in balance, we feel able to detach from subjective perceptions and we can see the symbolic truth and meaning in all situations as spiritually motivated for further learning and growth. Detachment is a huge part of opening the sixth energy center. It is here where we find our true path of service, our calling, and our meaningful contribution to life. We *feel* inspired, intuitive, positive, grateful, and very connected in spirit. We sense our true desire to serve and see with clarity and vision. We have divine insight.

Illness, seen from a sixth chakra perspective, often is the great motivator and transformer for us to turn inward and begin to understand higher truth and connection. The goal of becoming a conscious person is not to outwit or overcome our diseases, but to be able to handle whatever comes forth, without fear, and trust so we create mastery of the spirit. This is a HUGE concept and can be very difficult to actuallize. Becoming conscious in this center means letting go of what we think our life should be and embracing what is trying to work in our life, understanding that "all is well" is *always* in the big picture.

When imbalances occur in the sixth chakra, we feel disconnected and unenthusiastic about life. We sense no feeling of spiritual purpose, perpetuating a sense of separateness, heaviness, lethargy, and self-doubt. This fuels a "going nowhere" attitude that leads to hostility, envy, and fear. When there is no "greater purpose" in life, fear besieges us; fear of the past and future, fear of change or failure, fear of illness and death, and even fear of God and spirituality.

Destructive Patterns:

- "This is it. There is no more to life than waking and sleeping, waking and sleeping."
- "I am afraid."
- "My physical illnesses have nothing to do with how I live my life."
- "I'm not intuitive."
- "I don't have time to focus on prayer, meditation, or any of that stuff."
- "Intuition is nonsense. I get the facts and act on that ... period."

How to Begin Balancing the Sixth Chakra

There is a wonderful exercise called The Third Eye Meditation which is included in the exercise part of this book on page 182. It helps open the sixth center by focusing on higher consciousness and connection while breathing into the area between the brows. Taking time to meditate and focus on intuition each day will create opportunity to open this truth and wisdom center. Taking action on intuition is very important too. When we neglect to follow our intuition by refusing to act upon it, we discourage further insight, causing us to feel lost, uninspired, depressed, and unmotivated. This state is not the same as emotional depression, it is spiritual disconnection that can only be cured by listening and taking action on the feelings we have in our heart.

A LifeBreath session can create amazing transformation in the sixth chakra. I have seen people have life altering intuitive "hits" during and after a session. Their third eye may open and they receive information that helps transform their lives. For example, they may suddenly feel safe to explore a new job or confront someone whom they feel has been holding back their personal healing. They may let go of the past in order to embrace a new healthier future. When they take action on the messages they receive, their life may take quantum leaps towards higher purpose and a higher state of consciousness.

Lastly, take action…JUST DO IT.! I have seen people struggle over and over again because their intellect, fears, and overzealous sense of responsibility to others have stopped them from pursuing their passion. They are too frightened to trust. I have also seen people follow their dreams, no matter how crazy or impractical they seemed, and fly (mentally, physically, emotionally, spiritually, and financially). They just trusted and took a literal leap of faith. They jumped off the cliff and flew. And if they didn't fly, they fell, got back up, got a new challenge, flew, fell, got back up, and kept learning and listening until they figured it out. They saw each fall as a lesson to learn so that they could move forward in consciousness and connection. *Trust !!!*

Questions to Ask Yourself to Understand and Transform Your Sixth Chakra

- Am I judgmental?
- Do I listen to my intuition?
- Do I take time each day to grow my intuitive powers?
- What am I frightened of?
- What beliefs and attitudes would I like to change?
- Do I NOT act on new information and truths because it's too scary or too much work to change?
- Do I place trust in God's (spirit, nature, etc.) word to me and allow that to carry through to reality in my life? If not, why?
- Do I want to live a more conscious lifestyle, making it a priority, and if not, what is stopping me?

Affirmations for the Sixth Chakra

- The world does not hold power over me.
- I choose to listen to my inside world.
- My 6th chakra is open & balanced.
- I am compassionate.
- I trust my inner voice.
- I serve my higher power willingly.
- I am open to receiving intuition.

Chakra VII

7th Chakra

Focus: Spirit
    Divine Purpose/Destiny/Where Body & Spirit Fuse

Location: Crown

Color: Violet

Physiology: Genetics, Life-energy in general

Possible Associated Disorders:
    Genetic disorders,
    Life-Threatening Illnesses,
    Multiple Organs involved in
    any condition

Sacred Truth: *"Live in the present moment"*

Seventh Chakra Energy:

Spirit	Devotion	Mystical connection
Prophetic thought	Grace	Visions
Hope	True Healing	Source of miracles
Transcendence	Union with the Divine	Prayer

"The Soul is One with God." —Meister Echhart

"God is love, and he who is in love is in God and God in him." —unknown

Reminder: Breathe into your crown as you read this section in order to focus your energy to the seventh chakra.

The seventh chakra is where we connect to spirit. Often depicted as a halo, this center at the top of our head is the chakra of prayer, grace, devotion, inspiration, discipline (from the root word disciple), and the nature of goodness (God-ness). Miracles, grace, transcendence, and mystical connection evolve in this energy center.

When we are in alignment in our crown chakra, we feel forthright, fearless, responsible, and open hearted with a general sense of oneness with all. Our purest connection to the divine is poured through our crown which gives us access to the power of illumination and spiritual will. This serves as a bridge to a higher order beyond this reality so we may manifest energy as the will of the Higher Self. We become a spiritual instrument of expression and this helps teach us the right use of higher will. We feel connected and grateful, limitless and full of grace.

When we are not in alignment with our seventh energy center, we often have poor choices of will and feel detached and uninspired. We blame everyone and everything else for our failures, as well as for our successes. Life is outside of us rather than from within. We are often selfish, ungrateful, undisciplined, unfaithful, ungrounded or too grounded, and detached. We have no trust or faith in ourselves, others, or God. We begin defining the truth in self-serving ways. Life can feel overwhelming and unsatisfying. We are consciously or unconsciously fearful of most things in life, especially love, the future, and our own mortality.

All other chakra are aligned and balanced when the seventh center is completely open. True saints, masters, and prophets are open to the energy of the crown. The rest of us are working on opening into this energy as often as we can through unconditional love, conscious intention, and action. Fear and illusion close off the center. Love, forgiveness, and truth open it.

Destructive Patterns:

- "I am afraid."
- "I don't trust."
- "I never have enough (time, money, friends, power, stuff)."
- "I am afraid of a more meaningful life."
- "I am afraid of death."
- "I am afraid of life."

How to Begin Balancing the Seventh Chakra

- Make your spiritual devotion a priority.
- Give thanks daily.
- Believe in miracles.
- Believe in intuition.
- Pray.
- Meditate.
- Keep a "grace" bank account.
- Seek to overcome your fears.
- Find your passion in life and take action upon it.
- Listen to your intuition
- Give your life over to God, but at the same time, realize that you must meet him half way.
- BREATHE

Meditation and "crown breathing" will assist you in tapping into the energy of the universe so that you can align yourself with your higher purpose and true self-identity. (see "exercise" section). As you continue your practices, the calm and peace that you sense during meditation will automatically begin to enter into your daily life. Before you know it, life will become easier, more meaningful, and fulfilling.

The LifeBreath Technique has helped people find a sense of *"knowing."* During a session it is not uncommon for people to *feel* their chakra open, let go of old negative patterns, and sense spirit within them. Spiritual messages have come through images, voices, dreams, and visions. After a session, people have made cathartic transformation in their beliefs and actions.

LifeBreath helps open, align, and transform the energy in our body and beyond. Along with attention, intention, and action, this breathwork can manifest and expedite true transformation that leads to opening our life beyond our perceived limitations and into the realm of spiritual fulfillment and peace.

Questions to Ask Yourself to Understand and Transform Your Seventh Chakra

- What is my faith? What do I believe in?
- What is important to me (in the big picture)?
- What are my thoughts about the connection of illness, disease, life, and death?
- Do I make bargains with God?
- Do I accept where I am right now? Do I trust that I am always safe?
- How much does fear play a part of my life?
- Do I seek a deeper meaning to my life?

Affirmations for the Seventh Chakra

- I am.
- I am always safe.
- I follow my intuition.
- I am loved and loving.
- I am open.
- I am open to all possibilities. My Crown chakra is open & balanced.
- I am connected to my Higher Power.
- My spirit blesses me every day.
- I am connected with my highest good.

Common Restricted Breath Patterns in Everyday Life

Why We Learn Patterns of Restricted Breathing in the First Place

We each have a lifetime of experiences accumulated in our body and our natural breathing patterns. Our breathing is as normal and familiar to us as all our other daily functions. However, unlike many of our other physical functions, we can regulate our breathing through conscious effort and exercises. Breathing is the only function that is both conscious and subconscious, linking it to both our physical and emotional well being. Therefore, our experiences ultimately affect the quality of our breathing, but changing our breathing can change our experiences or at least how we perceive them. We store our experiences in our body and this directly affects our breathing. Our breath is an analogy to how we live. The way we breathe and the way we live are synonymous. The inhale represents our capacity to draw in the goodness of life and the exhale represents our ability to let go.

The Hawaiian word OHANA is used today to mean family. The older meaning literally meant, "People who breathe together." When missionaries came to the island they were called HAOLES, meaning, unflatteringly "people without breath." Sad, but true, when we lose our connection with breath, we lose association to our outer and inner worlds.

Let's get back to our baby's breath. Imagine observing the little belly; diaphragm, and chest lift gently outward on the inhale then gently inward on the exhale. The inhale flows without stopping into the exhale. The breath is gentle, natural, full, and beautiful. The breath of some adults can look a little more like World War III!!! So what happens?

There are many factors that contribute to restricted breathing patterns. These patterns create Physically, Emotionally, Mentally, and Spiritually uneasy energy flow that can cause *dis-ease*.

Societal Influences

Our parents and their parents before them did NOT get "Breathing 101" in primary school, not even in secondary school or college. Over the course of time, we have gotten away from nature and Breath. I can often see duplicated breathing patterns in mother/daughter and father/son relationships. Even different nationalities and ethnic groups have common breathing patterns. We naturally mimic our parents, friends, mentors, and heroes.

Modern Paradigm: Holding the Belly in to Look Thinner and Prevent Back Pain

Somewhere, somehow, someone decided that sucking your belly in makes you more attractive. I call it the Twiggy Syndrome. Young and old alike, we are bombarded with media that attacks our uniqueness and even our basic right to be healthy. Here are a few of the culprits:

Tight Pants	Belts	High Heels	Bras
Neck Ties	Girdles	Tight Panties	Stockings

There is a notion that by holding our abdominal muscles in tight, we support our back and prevent back pain. This is incorrect. Constantly tightening abdominal muscles actually increases tension and stiffness. Oscillation of the breath increases blood flow and creates movement in the spine, making for a healthier back.

Ignorance

The average person just doesn't know any better. We often figure that one day we *get born* and breathe and another day we *get dead* and stop breathing – and that's all there is to it. However, our breath is a direct analogy to how we live our life. Education and good habit building are essential.

Habit

Restrictive breathing patterns simply can be bad habits. Once you are taught "good breathing," your life force will grow stronger *(This sounds like Yoda talking to Sky Walker. "May the **force** be with you.")*.

Poor Posture

Poor posture restricts our breathing. Because our breathing is not full, radiant, unobstructed and peaceful, neither are our lives.

Fight or Flight Response

Cavemen and women needed it as a survival tool. Animals use it each day to stay alive. But the fight or flight response overwhelms and plagues modern man through overuse and getting stuck in it.

Your heart begins to pound, your body's energy is directed into the essential organs, your belly tightens, you freeze, and your respiration quickens and shifts into hysterical chest breathing. Is it your killer? Is it an animal ready to attack you? No, it's just that your pain in the butt boss walked into the room! So now you might stay in panic mode for minutes, hours or days. You might even be STUCK in fight or flight permanently because you don't know any differently.

(Don't worry, I'm going to teach you how to get unstuck.)

Physical Trauma *(especially in abdominal or lower back region)* and Pain

If you are hurt, that physical trauma can stay in your body forever. Your breathing can change forever.

Notice how you breathe when you are in pain. You usually hold your breath, not only in the area of the pain (if it's where you breathe) but also in other areas. For instance, when your lower back is hurting, you'll tend to hold your breath almost everywhere. This is because holding your breath numbs you to the pain. Breath makes you feel, and holding your breath is a type of natural anaesthetic. The problem seems to be twofold. First, when you restrict your breath in a certain area, that area no longer gets the benefit of the energy that breath brings. That's why it is best to b-r-e-a-t-h-e into an area that is distressed. Secondly, the restrictive pattern becomes habitual. You continue to hold your breath even after you are out of pain.

Learning to breathe into an area or through a painful experience can decrease the immediate pain and also decrease the long lasting effects of the trauma.

Emotional Trauma

Picture yourself being yelled at (either now or as a child). I can feel myself holding my breath, not wanting to feel awful and ashamed (again). I hold back the tears, my stomach and head hurts, my throat swells. Our natural response to emotional trauma can affect all of our body's systems. In general, we shut down our breathing, like we do with physical trauma, like an anaesthetic. When things hurt too badly, we may shut our breathing off almost completely. Breathwork can directly access the wounds, opening and rebalancing both old and new physical and emotional trauma.

Restricted Breath Patterns 101

Early on, while observing thousands of people's breathing, I began noticing common patterns of restriction. I can both see and feel these patterns and they are directly associated Physically, Emotionally, Mentally, and Spiritually with the energy around the restricted area and the chakras. For example, a restriction in the chest is often associated with emotions of the heart – love, compassion, self-love, and nurturing, whereas a restriction in the diaphragm is often about fear and power. The specific dynamics of the breathing patterns would tell me what the pattern meant.

In studying vibrational medicine and Einstein's theories on matter and energy, I became aware that uneasiness and disease shows up *first* in our energy field and *then* in our physical body. It may even show up in our breathing **before** our body! Because energy and matter are interchangeable, resolving restrictive breathing patterns can be done either by changing the cause of the pattern or by changing the breathing pattern itself.

(We will look at this more specifically when we cover "Breathing Analysis" in the LifeBreath section.)

Chest Breathing

This breathing pattern occurs when the abdomen is tightly held inward which prevents the diaphragm from descending, in order to take a full inhale, or even ascending completely during an exhale. These people never seem to get enough air, consciously or subconsciously, which makes them fight even harder for their next breath. When asked to take a deep breath, they puff up like a frog and use their upper chest, upper back, shoulders, and neck muscles to breathe. This causes constant tension in the abdomen from sucking in, and in the chest, back, neck, and shoulders from being overworked and physically tensed.

This pattern can be attributed to many factors. We often follow our role models and many super-heroes, both male and female, stick out their chests and pull in their bellies. We may also simply follow the patterns of those around us. In order to feel or look thinner people hold their muscles in. Men sometime stick out their chests to feel stronger or look more dangerous. Unfortunately, by tensing the abdomen the circulation is stifled and the organs do not get the oxygen nor the energy they need to flourish. The tightened upper body creates tension in the heart and lungs as well. Hypertension, heart disease, poor blood circulation, organ disease, low back problems, chronic tension, and menstrual cycle problems are a few of the physical manifestations of chest breathing.

Of course, there are the emotional reasons for tensing and not breathing into the abdomen. After all, we hold so many emotions below the heart and in order to disconnect with those feelings, we stop breathing there and even hold our "stuff" down there with tension. It is very common for people who have been abused to not breathe very low into the belly. And because the chest breather has to work so hard at breathing, they often perceive life as hard work. Anxiety, nervousness, poor self-esteem, and poor self image are common in people who chest breathe due to emotional repression.

Gasping for breath is a form of chest breathing. Simply put, this person gasps for air; the inhale is dramatic and severe. They have gotten in the habit of contracting the diaphragm in a quick, short impulse. This does not allow the breath to extend below the solar plexus, keeping it in the chest. This gasping may represent extreme grasping for many of the good things in life and also add health risks to upper chest breathing.

There are modalities of exercise that profess a constant inward pull for an erect spine and body alignment. However, the spine and body can be erect and aligned beautifully without that constant tension. Physical tension creates emotional tension and it is unhealthy to practice contractive styles of breathwork for every day living. This should be left to what I call "special occasion" breathing, where we are trying for a certain response from an exercise.

Concave Breathing

This is another form of chest breathing, but with a very different posturing. The body is collapsed over itself with rounded shoulders and the neck, hips, and belly are forward. The whole body is C-shaped or concave. The person looks tired, hunched, and old. The breath never makes it to the lower lungs or even the upper lungs because of their poor posture.

Basically, there is very little breath moving in either direction, so the concave breather is often tired, lethargic, and lazy. The whole body is sub-ventilated and the tolls will be paid, Physically, Emotionally, Mentally, and Spiritually. All the physical functions in the body will be labored. The spine is collapsed and years of hunching will create permanent damage. The resulting oxygen depravation will affect mental stability and capability. Longevity or being energetic and healthy does not look good for this shallow breather.

I have never seen a concave breather who is confident or energetic, most likely, they have seen severe trauma, abuse, and have a horrendously poor self image. I see the beginning of concave breathing in many of our young ladies of today, especially teenagers. It's as though they are ashamed of the form their new bodies are taking and in order to hide it, they hunch. They also often subdue their breathing in order to not fully feel.

Convex Breathing

Convex breathing is a little different then chest breathing. It is sticking your solar plexus out beyond the rest of your body (beyond the shoulders, chest and hips). One day my husband and I were at the New Jersey boardwalk and we saw a young man walking by who had the most pronounced diaphragm we had ever seen. He looked like a giant backwards C. He was strutting like a rooster trying to impress the young ladies around him. He too, would have very shallow breathing because he was not only chest breathing and holding in the abdomen, but he was also holding tension *everywhere* (jaw, neck, shoulders, chest, abdomin, back, and even his butt)!

This type of breathing can have the same ill effects as concave breathing, but with the added ramifications of tension. And although it may not seem like it, when you meet a convex breather, their confidence is likely to be poor, with their puffed out chests overcompensating for their low self image.

Reverse Breathing

During natural diaphragmatic breathing, the abdomen extends outward, away from the spine during the inhale, and it falls toward the spine on the exhale. I liken it to a balloon filling with air and releasing air on the inhale and exhale, respectfully. We don't push out with the muscles to extend the belly, it just naturally occurs when the lower lungs are filled and the diaphragm is extended.

During reverse breathing, just the opposite occurs. The person's abdomen pulls inward during the inhale and outward during the exhale. This may occur from wearing tight clothing, habitually pulling inward to look thinner, perceived societal norms, or emotional/ physical trauma.

Reverse breathers are often "not in their bodies." They are sometimes clumsy and have difficulty learning physical skills. They may live in a state of confusion and disorientation. And because the breath is not moving through the lower chakras, illness around the midsection is common. The massaging motion of good abdominal breathing is not present so the lower organs are disturbed energetically. Chronic muscle tension around the shoulders, neck, and upper back occur because they are using the smaller secondary muscles to breathe, rather than the stronger, larger primary muscles including the diaphragm. I have witnessed many cancer patients who are reverse breathers and sub-ventilators. Sometimes reverse breathing is sporadic which creates even more confusion and hysteria.

Shallow or No Breathing - Subventilating

Imagine being scared half to death. You initially take a gasp, then your body freezes up and you hold your breath and wait. What if you keep waiting and waiting and get stuck in this frozen dilemma? There are people who can barely take a breath. When I guide them to take a nice relaxed BIG breath, I can hardly see movement in any part of their body. It's as though they are half dead, and unfortunately, energetically, they are. Being physically ill can cause this type of breathing. On the other hand, having a traumatic history can cause it as well (which can turn into physical illness later).

Shallow breathing has been linked to dozens of physical, emotional, and mental disorders through valid scientific research. Americans and people throughout the world are shallow breathers. It is not surprising that chronic diseases are overunning our healthcare systems.

Working with someone who has little or no breathing is extremely interesting. Often, I must be very gentle and start with simple chi kung movements and breath. When I introduce the LifeBreath Technique, it is in small controlled sessions. As the breather works on the emotional trauma that seized up their breathing in the first place, the breath begins to open as well. The changes in personality, energy and overall well-being are amazing.

Breath Holding

After the exhale phase there can be a slight natural pause during normal breathing. Some mystics claim it is there where the "nothingness" of the meditative mind connects to "all there is." It is definitely a place of calm and altered states of consciousness. However, when we hold our breath because of stress and tension, problems arise. Did you ever take notice of how often you hold your breath throughout a day? It can be due to bad habits, physical pain, stress, and/or emotional suppression.

Simply stated, holding onto the inhale or exhale stressfully is a bad habit and causes tension. When we are holding our breath under tension, we are not bringing in oxygen or exhaling carbon monoxide. Less energy, increased tension and more toxins equals poorer health, Physically, Emotionally, Mentally, and Spiritually (PEMS).

Contractive or Tension Breathing

This type of breathing can be related to any of the breath patterns, but includes tensing, pressure or pushing anywhere throughout the inhale, exhale, or pauses. This pattern represents some sort of struggle. Contraction on the inhale is connected to difficulties "breathing in the good stuff in life." Contraction on the exhale represents the inability to "let go", surrender, and "just be." Pain, both physical and emotional, can restrict our breathing. Mental anxiety represses our breath patterns. Spiritual disconnection and feeling "uninspired" makes us breathe less.

Throat tension is a kind of contractive breathing. The breath gets stuck in the throat. We have all felt that tension of throat holding when we are overwhelmed or emotionally upset. I get it every time I hear a great rendition of the American Anthem or watch Little House on the Prairie. When we get stuck in this tension, however, it blocks the entire breath from going deeper and it also suppresses emotions trying to work their way up and out. Chronic jaw tension, neck pressure, tightened vocal cords, and headaches are common manifestations of tension breathing.

Hyperventilation and The Fight or Flight Response

At the opposite end of the breathing spectrum from relaxed, full, belly breathing is hyperventilation. Most people know hyperventilation as extremely rapid or deep breathing that over-oxygenates the blood, causing dizziness or fainting.

Hyperventilaters breathe rapidly no matter what they are doing, exchanging short rapid breaths for longer expanded breaths in order to compensate for lack of oxygen. Getting caught in hyperventilation breathing consistently is very unhealthy. Once again, there are PEMS causative agents.

> *"If you started to hyperventilate in a doctor's office, he or she would probably have you breathe into a paper bag, saturating your blood with carbon dioxide and restoring balance. If you started to hyperventilate in my office, I would invite you to contact the emotion you were concealing and breathe into it. After a few deep belly-breaths into the fear, anger, or sadness, you would probably have a release of the emotion and feel better than you did before. I say this with some confidence because I have witnessed this same sequence hundreds of times. There is usually an emotional trigger that starts the hyperventilation. If you can identify and deal with the emotion, the hyperventilation fades quickly."*
>
> —Gay Hendricks, about hyperventilation from his book, <u>Conscious Breathing</u>.

During the times that we "perceive" danger, our body goes on high alert and into the fright or flight response for survival.

The process looks like this…

- Our body readies to fight.
- Our abdominal muscles tighten.
- Our breath shifts to upper chest breathing.
- Adrenaline shoots into the bloodstream. (slowing digestion, shifting energy into our muscles to use to fight or run)
- We may shift from nostril breathing to mouth breathing for more oxygen.
- We may hyperventilate.

The problem begins in getting stuck in the fight or flight response. Staying in this hyperventilated state on a long term basis may create conditions of fatigue, exhaustion, heart palpitations, rapid pulse, dizziness, visual disturbances, shortness of breath, yawning, chest pains, headaches, tension, muscles cramps, stomach pain, muscle pain, anxiety, insomnia, nightmares, and tingling and pressure in the extremities, described by physicians as tetany. Most people don't know they are hyperventilating. It can be very subtle and also chronic. There are different levels of short rapid breathing. Elongating your breath and taking fewer breaths per minute induces the *Relaxation Response* which can have extreme health benefits that counteract hyperventilation.

Anything below fifteen breaths per minute is usually considered healthy breathing. This has a direct and immediate connection with our stress level. Anything above this may be considered restricted. Dr. Robert Fried, in his book, The Breath Connection, suggests men usually breathe about 12 –14 beats per minute and women tend to breathe about 14 – 15 beats per minute.

Hyperventilation is a breathing pattern above these numbers where there are acid/alkaline and carbon dioxide imbalances in the body. This shifts the chemical reactions in the cells and according to Dr. Fried, causes less oxygen to be carried to the cells than we need, causing dizziness and breathlessness. The arteries constrict, resulting in low blood flow into the extremities causing cold hands and feet. Muscle tension may occur from a build up of calcium in the muscles and nerves making them hyperactive. The nervous system becomes overwhelmed, making us a host for irritability and overreaction. Emotionally, hyperventilaters may feel varying levels of anxiety, hysteria, nervousness and hyper-ness. This may feel normal to a hyperventilater. But once we can get them relaxed and to elongate their breath, they can sense the new higher level of *normal* in their lives.

When I was in my early twenties I lived in New Mexico. The first week we lived there we went backpacking on top of Wheeler Peak, the highest mountain in the area. Unfortunately, I got altitude sickness. I was nauseous, breathless, my hands and feet become numb, and I had the worst sledge hammer headache of my life. I was also extremely irritable. I ended up going to sleep on the trail further down while everyone ascended to the coveted peak. The numbness that I felt in my extremities is called tetany and is a side effect of hyperventilation. Tingling, muscle tightness, and even muscle pain are common with tetany. These sensations can be mild, but they can also be very intense.

As a side note, many people SUB-ventilate. They become lethargic and suffer the ills of restricted energy throughout their PEMS systems. To them, this is normal. Hyperventilation could actually be a cure for sub-ventilation.

Combination Breathing

We all experience some breathing restrictions. Throughout our life many things happen; as we experience life and change, our breathing patterns will change. We may experience combinations of the different breaths. If you are going through something very traumatic or working through past, you may experience shallow breathing, holding your breath, no belly breath, and even hyperventilation during especially overwhelming times or any combination thereof.

Where do I Breathe?

Exercise

Ask yourself::

- Where do I breathe? Where don't I breathe?
  Low abdomen, abdomen, solar plexus, low chest, high chest, back, neck, shoulders?

- Where does my breath originate?
  Low, high, center?

- How often do I inhale and exhale?

- What is the relationship of my inhale to my exhale?
  How long is my inhale compared to my exhale?

- Is my breath smooth and even? Or cumbersome and uneven?

- Are there places my breath feels restricted, tight, or difficult?

- What is the quality of my breath?
  (try using some adjectives like easy or hard, flowing or abrupt)

- Do I have pauses? Are the pauses relaxed and light or tense and long?

- Are there places where I struggle for breath?

- Do I hold my breath? Why?

- What does my breath feel like during different times of the day or week according to what I am doing and thinking, who I am with and where I am?

As we continue to experience conscious, full, diaphragmatic belly breathing, keep these questions in mind and "tweak" your breathing until it feels full and easy. And as you work through your life experiences and continue to shift and transform, call upon your breathing as your special tool that manifests peace, joy, and personal power.

Breathwork with Special Populations

Birth, Newborns and Children

Pregnant women, newborns, and children of any age can benefit from conscious breathing and the LifeBreath Technique.

First, during pregnancy, it is not only recommended to learn Breathwork for pain management for delivery, it is has absolutely wonderful benefits for both the mother and the baby throughout the entire pregnancy. Drawing in deeper, more relaxed breath helps oxygenate the fetus. Everyday full breathing will keep the mother calm and relaxed and elicit the *Relaxation Response*, which can lower blood pressure and heart rate.

During a LifeBreath session, the mother can learn to let go of the past and future and really focus on the here and now with a renewed sense of energy and flow. An incredible connection can occur during a session between the mother and baby. It is very common for a baby to become extremely active during the session and for the mother to feel a great sense of peace and joy.

During delivery, Lamaze breathing has worked very well for women all over the world. I encourage women and a partner to learn Lamaze breathing and/or the LifeBreath Technique. If I had my deliveries to do over again, I would bring the baby to my heart and do LifeBreath with him/her immediately after delivery. The baby will feel the immediate rising and falling of my breath, my heart beat and also feel my love. The baby will often begin to naturally take on the breath of its mother. This whole process assists in the baby's birth trauma. *Think about it, the baby went from a perfectly temperate, loving environment to… cold, intense light, breathing for the first time on his or her own, painful eyedrops, and a bunch of strangers.*

Throughout infancy the baby can be "Breathed" any time, just by placing him or her on your chest while YOU breathe. The child will automatically feel your breath and your energy and they will react to it. *Try it, it's incredible.*

As the child gets older, you can either breathe with them chest to chest by laying side by side, or you can "spoon" them and sit or lay your chest to their back. Eventually, when they understand the words, you can teach them how to breathe. It is especially helpful when a child becomes physically or emotionally distressed. You can immediately scoop them up and breathe with them. They will begin to automatically begin to breathe when they feel the need. And, don't forget to teach your children to become habitual belly breathers so they don't have to be untaught later. It will help them to be healthier and happier all on levels of life.

> *"I strongly suspect that all children engage in "advanced" breathing/healing practices, only to forget them as the habits of age literally take the breath away."*
> —Michael Sky, <u>Breathing.</u>

Think about how infants and children feel emotions. They feel sadness or anger or joy fully, then they let it go completely and move on. *Maybe it is we who should learn from them.*

You can teach children to continue to feel their emotions in the present moment, breathe when things feel overwhelming or constricting, and to become a conscious breather and a conscious, loving person.

Pain Relief

The pain-relieving effects of breathwork have been used by childbirth coaches to help mothers through labor for decades. Now a number of other medical professionals, including dentists, are using breathing to help patients control pain. Because the *Relaxation Response* is connected to our breathing, when we consciously breathe for pain relief, it relaxes the body, dampens the feeling of pain and we feel less intensity. Using the LifeBreath Technique may also help find the *cause* of the pain and work on a cellular level to release the pain.

Stress Management

Breathwork and meditation join together to create the optimal environment for the *Relaxation Response*. Stress has been proven to be one of the leading factors of many, if not most, physical and psychological disorders.

Anger Management

Count to ten. Take a few deep breaths. Leading experts agree that anger can be managed. Through conscious intention, shifting one's paradigm, and taking a few deep breaths, anger can be shifted. Eventually, if on the right path, anger can even be alleviated.

Menopause

It has been proven that breathwork can lessen hot flashes, mood swings, and other menopausal symptoms. The LifeBreath Technique is a powerful resource for passing through the changes with few problems.

Teenagers

A most challenging stage of life, adolescence can not only be difficult, but transformational, and it is a springboard for the rest of life. My experiences with teenagers have been awesome. I have found them to be open and looking for experiential opportunities. They are often looking for altered states of mind, but not always in a positive light. LifeBreath gives them a very positive tool for altered states of consciousness, expression, transformation, emotional and mental clarity, and a positive self-supported spiritual path to follow. Unlike drugs and alcohol, LifeBreath and other conscious breathing techniques are healthy and both physically and energetically supportive.

Youngsters

Young people are very open to learning to breathe. I have been teaching breathwork to groups of children from the age of four to fourteen for years. They love to breathe and they instantly feel the positive consequences of their breathing. We use it in our Martial Arts classes to help teach focus and clarity, and to help create physical power, stamina, and speed.

The LifeBreath Technique, used in short spurts, enables youngsters to learn, early on, that breath can be used for PEMS well-being.

ADHD

We are seeing a growing number of ADD and ADHD cases in our public schools. In my own Martial Arts classes the numbers are staggering. Where I use to have two or three hyperactive children per year, now I see three or four per class! There is no doubt in my mind that LifeBreath assists the children in learning to manage their attention spans. This also gives them a self-help tool to assist them to create a better life. For example, after participating in a fifteen minute LifeBreath session, a sixth grader with ADHD was able to write a cohesive page description on his experience without assistance. His usual ADHD behavior disappeared for the day. After a short LifeBreath session, most of our karate students' behavior improves drastically. I see the benefits in both my adult and children students.

Cancer

I have worked with many cancer patients and found that LifeBreath brings a profound sense of well-being and connection for those who are ready to accept it. Interestingly, research has found the cancer can not live in an oxygen rich environment and that's good news. Someday, perhaps we will find that oxygen and breathing are a piece to the cancer mystery. In the meantime, we can continue using breathwork to help promote PEMS balancing.

> *Here's very interesting research:*
>
> "The first discovery was made by Nobel Price winner, Dr. Otto Warburg, Director of the Max Planck Institute for Cell Physiology in Berlin. He confirmed that the key precondition for the development of cancer is a lack of oxygen at the cellular level."
>
> —Nathaniel Altman, <u>Oxygen Healing Therapies</u>.

Heart Disease

It has also been proven that conscious breathing can help heart patients. There are exercises that I do in my Chi Kung classes that stimulate the heart through movement and breathing. The exercises also massage the organs and oxygenate the blood more fully. This form of exercise relieves stress and anxiety, which has been proven to decrease the rate of heart disease and heart attack. The LifeBreath Technique can also work on a cellular level to stimulate your own immune system, health, and healing.

Functional Breathing Disorders

Asthma, chronic bronchitis, aphonia (loss of voice due to hysteria), diseased or traumatized larynx, chronic laryngitis, sinusitis, emphysema, hyperventilation, and pneumonia are all classified as respiratory system diseases. It just makes sense that when we learn to breathe more effectively and efficiently, it will support the function of our respiratory system.

I have worked with many asthmatics and we have actually not only helped their breathing, but have alleviated the need for many medications. Because of the emotional and mental aspects of being unable to breathe, LifeBreath has been extremely helpful in getting to the core cause of the inability to breathe. Studies show that diaphragmatic, or belly, breathing helps asthma patients breathe easier, which also helps them reduce the number of trips they make to the emergency room because of severe attacks, which could even result in death.

Singers

People who learn to sing correctly are usually very good diaphragmatic breathers. They have a very good handle on using the diaphragm in order to create better, longer sound. When working with singers, I have found two recurring issues that we work on. First, they forget to bring the belly breathing into their everyday life. Second, we usually need to work on getting their breath up into their upper lungs more. They're often great in the belly, but need work in the chest.

Breathwork for Athletes

"Your breathing determines whether you are at your best or whether you are at a disadvantage."
—Carola H. Speads

"I use LifeBreath to prepare me for competing as a marathon runner." —LL

"When I do a short LifeBreath session before Karate class, I am ON!" —JB

Good health is created on a foundation of correct breathing and there are many proven physical benefits to full, effective breathing for athletes. Athletes benefit as much as lay people. They receive more energy for life in general. There is more energy for physical training, faster recovery, and better concentration and focus. Breathwork reduces stress, which promotes more consistent training. There is a maximum blood flow to the muscles, making workouts more effective and efficient. The increased oxygen in the blood creates better strength and endurance training. The more efficient clearing of toxins helps with faster recovery after training and works with the lymphatic system. There is an overall sense of physical energy before, during, and after training.

I have been a personal trainer for over fifteen years, and have found that teaching my clients how to breathe is essential for their overall health. It is amazing to see how many people hold their breath while being involved in physical activities. Without realizing it, people who unconsciously don't breathe are shutting off their lifeline. To go even further, by breath-holding, they are causing pressure and tension to build. This can be very unhealthy and even lead to aneurysms and premature death.

There are techniques in weight training where you hold your breath and create thoracic tension. This is a viable tool, but should be used sparingly and with a good base knowledge so as not to create too much pressure.

Learning to exhale during exertion and inhale beforehand is simple but great advice. Tennis, golf, baseball, gymnastics, martial arts, track and field, crew, basketball, football – all participants in sports can benefit from sport specific breathing techniques.

Breathwork also helps athletes on a very different level. It aids in the athletes' ability to handle stress, stay centered, and play or practice at their best. When I watch someone like Tiger Woods or a great tennis player or football player, they are in "the zone." They play better than they ever have when they are centered and relaxed, and their talents come out naturally after years of practice. These athletes may or may not have the best natural talent, strength, skills, or speed in the world, but because they can "keep it all together" they consistently win. I bet anything, these people *breathe*.

Lois Hayes

It may be a good time to mention Lois Hayes' work. She has beautifully systemized the cause and effect of negative thinking and a demented belief system in her book, <u>You Can Heal Yourself</u>. She correlates a particular thought to a particular ailment that is quite literal in the body. For instance, a problem in a joint may carry energy around feeling unsupported. Asthma can correspond to a feeling of being suffocated. Diabetes plays with the idea of not being able to see the sweetness in life. Although I believe in the 70/30 rule that about 70 percent of our ailments are both preventable and mentally/emotionally/spiritually based, it's very interesting work and I highly recommend the book. Her ideas, in my opinion, correlate significantly to a person's breathing patterns.

Section II

The

LifeBreath

Technique

LifeBreath

In Section I, we examined the many benefits of LifeBreath and full conscious breathing. The LifeBreath Technique expedites and enhances our well-being more profoundly than any other Breathwork I have ever experienced. Unto itself, it can be experientially cathartic, but on a day to day level, it assists in creating healthy breathing patterns that are less restrictive and more supportive of optimal health and radiant living.

The LifeBreath Technique focuses on a full, robust, active breath that waves from the lower abdomen towards the upper chest. It can be very active, with varying speeds and intensities. The inhale represents all the good in life along with our ability to accept it. The exhale relates to our ability to let go and how we handle struggle and negativity.

LifeBreath's foundation lies in the fact that ALL people need to learn to *BREATHE* more fully, so they can learn to *LIVE* more fully.

Let's not make our breathing necessarily right or wrong, just more or less open or restricted in effectively assisting us in an upward spiral in our life journey. As we embark through LifeBreath sessions we are ever-changing. Each session and each person's breathing takes on its own personality and individual attributibutes. During parts of the session, we may consciously control our breathing, but often, quite amazingly, the breath takes on its own patterns, guiding us where we need to go. Every session is perfect in that it gives us exactly what we need, *even though we may not know it at the time.* The Breath does not necessarily change the way we feel, it enables us to feel what we already feel in greater detail. Whatever stands out emotionally in our life, stands out during Breath.

LifeBreath helps open and clear restricted breathing and it teaches you how to more efficiently and easily breathe. It helps us learn why we shut our breathing down in the first place and then we can move on to a more spiritual understanding of life.

LifeBreath is versatile, pleasurable, portable, autonomous, extremely simple, and efficient.

LifeBreath works on these four basic levels:
Physically, Emotionally, Mentally, and Spiritually

Physically, LifeBreath helps detoxify and energize the body. It allows us to create and balance chi flow.

Emotionally, it helps integrate old feelings that are contracted in our body and energy field. It helps us find peace and truly expedites our transformational process.

Mentally, we can create great clarity, vision, focus, and change.

Spiritually, LifeBreath becomes a very powerful tool on our journey towards profound spiritual fulfillment.

"He lives most life whoever breathes most air."
—Elizabeth Barrett Browning

"Our breath is the fragile vessel that carries us from birth to death."
—Dr. Frederick Leboyer

"We are children of breath, and the way is ever open for our return to a life divine and everlasting."
—Michael Sky

Quotes by LifeBreath Practitioners

Practitioners of the LifeBreath Technique are almost always taken aback by how powerfully this breathwork affects their lives. Here's what a few of them have to say…

LifeBreath is…

- A powerful self-help tool that helped resolve my personal problems
- A physical cleansing
- A mental balancing tool
- Energizing
- Energy that nourishes the body, mind, and spirit
- A jump start for your metabolism
- Strengthening my sexual energy
- Creative energy
- A way to better health
- A spiritual connection
- A conduit for deeper levels of consciousness
- An emotional letting go
- Fun and experiential
- Easy to learn
- Self-empowering and making me strong on all levels
- A transformational tool like no other
- Life altering
- Making me laugh again
- For everyone
- Connecting me to aspects of my Higher Self
- Something I can always do for myself
- Helping me become whole again
- Helped me deal with grief, depression, and turmoil in my life
- Life force running through my veins
- Helping me break my old bad habits and my addictions
- About letting go of the past and living in the moment
- Something I love to do in a group or alone
- A stress reducer
- Helping me through hard times
- Sometimes it isn't easy, but it's ALWAYS worthwhile
- Helping me love myself again

LifeBreath is … Love … Joy … Radiant Health … Peace … A Blessing

> *"LifeBreath has changed my life in every way.*
> *I don't know what I would do without it."*
> —MR

"Dear Beth, I know this may seem a little late to send a thank you, but I was never quite certain about what to send or how to say what was necessary. It may not sound strange to you, but I completely underestimated the power of a breath session. After only practicing the breathing style for a month, I have changed my thought patterns. I feel happy almost all the time. I sleep better ... Since the second breathing session, I'm calmer and more peaceful, my past seems to be losing its power as the future continues to grow. Thank you for the introduction to peace of mind and heart; it's truly a wonderful feeling – freedom ... My goal of personal best and peace of mind and spirit seem much more accessible now. Thank you again." —MM

"I have had four heart attacks. I truly believe that LifeBreath came into my life to help me to learn how to relax, let go, and gain back my health. I have not had an attack since doing LifeBreath and my doctor can't believe my recovery. He says he doesn't know what the heck I'm doing, but just keep doing it." —SM

"I haven't used my asthma inhaler since I did my first breath session." —DS

"I lost ten pounds. I think it's because through my LifeBreath sessions I am relearning how to take care of myself. My self image is definitely improving and everyone is noticing." —DS

"Dear Beth,

I continue to sing the praises of Breathwork and how beneficial it is in my life. My testimonial is this: Before I started breathing, I had alot of issues, fears, uncertainties, along with just not feeling healthy, no energy. I also dealt with addictive problems.

One day my boyfriend told me about a breath session that was to be held at his Karate school that week and invited me! I had never heard anything about this before, but I figured I'd give it a try. It certainly couldn't hurt. I went without any expectations. The experience was very surprising too.

Some emotions came up that I thought were long gone. But at the end of the session I felt so peaceful yet full of energy. I want more of this, so I continued with unexpected results.

> *So, I took it further and traveled from NJ to Maine to train under Beth at the LifeBreath Institute. My life has done a one hundred eighty degree. I am a very peaceful person within today. The issues I dealt with through breathwork are either gone or acceptable and no longer rule me! This has, in turn, enabled me to move forward in my life in a way that I never thought possible. Thank you."* —SN

We now know that diaphragmatic breathing stimulates and massages our organs. It also tones the diaphragm and abdominal muscles. But the LifeBreath Technique super-oxygenates, revitalizes, cleanses, and exercises the organ systems by breathing even more deeply. Because so much of our emotional experience is registered in the abdomen, diaphragm, chest, and throat, LifeBreath assists in releasing the tension and repressed energy.

Dysfunctional breathing reinforces chronic tension and does not allow for full respiration. It's a "chicken and egg" scenario: repressed energy creates poor breathing AND poor breathing creates repressed energy. Through the work we do with the LifeBreath Technique, we can transform old patterns and create new healthier ones.

LifeBreath is used to expedite the process of transformation by directly increasing chi flow and creating intention for change and personal power.

After facilitating LifeBreath sessions for thousands of people, these benefits have been brought to my attention. These are simply the *"things"* I have witnessed.

- Increases energy and vitality
- Detoxifies the body
- Clears out old, unhealthy emotional patterns
- Creates clarity and harmony
- Strengthens the body. Strengthens the mind. Helps integrate emotions.
- Helps create and balance chi flow
- Strengthens the spirit
- Creates peace and balance
- Reduces stress and allows us to fully feel joy
- Creates a system to deal with stress and unhealthy emotional patterns
- Creates a system to assist healing addictive patterns
- Assists in abundance reprogramming
- People become happier and more productive with a greater sense of well being
- People let go of abusive relationships
- Family members become closer
- Increases athletic performance
- Increases respiratory ability
- Helps people feel better about themselves which helps them lose weight
- Medications no longer needed
- Asthmatic symptoms alleviated

- Increased ability to heal
- Helps to connect you more fully to life!

(We make no claims for your personal experience)

How It's Done

> *"I had the hardest time learning to breathe low in my abdomen. I had held my stomach in my whole life! Beth worked with me and I finally got it. Wow. Can you believe I breathed that way all those years? And, man, did it take a toll on my body. I had low back pain and a hysterectomy before I was thirty-five. I practice every day and I feel wonderful."*
> —DC

> *"Learning to breathe correctly has made me feel so much better. I use LifeBreath all day long to remind myself to breathe in my belly and up to my heart. It calms me, makes me more alert, and gives me more energy to do the things I love."*
> —SS

During a LifeBreath session, we usually begin by breathing in and out through a wide open mouth, about the size of a half dollar, with the jaw completely relaxed. The reasons I encourage mouth breathing to begin with are twofold. The first is very simple; your mouth hole is bigger than your nostrils, so you get more air, more life energy. The second reason has to do with our chakras. When you breathe through your mouth, you access your lower chakras. This is the area where we hold a lot of our *emotional luggage*, and that's one of the primary benefits of practicing LifeBreath, *letting go.*

The components of the actual breathing pattern are:
- In and out through the mouth.
- A fairly large and robust, non-stressful, relaxed breath.
- No pauses between the inhale and the exhale.
- The breath begins low in the torso, near the pubic bone.
- The breath flows upward towards the diaphragm, heart, shoulders, throat, and mouth.
- The breath is like a giant sign of infinity, a figure eight…circular.
- Most of the emphasis and work is done on the inhale.
- The body is completely relaxed – allowing "surrender," "letting go."
- The inhale is like a big yawn.
- The exhale is like a giant sigh, it is not forced nor blown out.
- The mouth stays open and relaxed through the inhale and exhale.
- A full open breath is best, large and unrestricted, but not overbearing or strained.

LifeBreath can also be performed through the nose. Our new "Natural Everyday Breathing" that we learned in Section I is LifeBreath done through the nostrils. In other words, full, belly to heart, relaxed, and circular breathing is our "Natural LifeBreath" style breathing (see "The Nine Keys to Healthy Normal Breathing"). Meditative breathing is usually done through the nose as well. We use nostril breathing during a Breath session to address the higher chakras. However, during the beginning stages of a LifeBreath session I encourage fuller, more rapid breathing than in every day breathing.

There are three basic breathing patterns:

    Easy and Full   Intense and Full   Intense and Shallow

We usually begin a LifeBreath session with "Easy and Full" breaths. This ignites the session with abundant amounts of life energy. It opens the breathing pattern and the breathers' Physical, Emotional, Mental, and Spiritual systems. As the person relaxes into the breathing, the volume of air intake increases and the more rapidly he or she begins to integrate thoughts and energy as they arise.

The "Intense and Full" breaths bring in greater amounts of air and more awareness to physical sensations. The inhale is drawn in just before a full exhale. In other words, you leave a little air in the lungs after the exhale and immediately begin the next inhale. The exhale is completely relaxed. If the inhale and exhale remain relaxed, the energy flows radiantly through the body. We can quicken the pace of breathing to expedite the transformation process. If there is tension, which is caused by resistance and restrictions, physical sensations are usually present and they can range from fairly light to very intense. We speed up the breathing pattern when feelings come up that are uncomfortable. We slow the breathing down when there are feelings of pleasure and bliss, bathing in the ecstacy. This often occurs naturally and automatically.

When the intensity is turned up, the "Intense and Shallow" pattern can be used to regulate the energy intake and slow perception of any physical and emotional discomfort. Intense, shallow breathing helps integrate difficult experiences.

Remember: Open mouth LifeBreath is only done for what I call "special occasion breathing." There is one exception to this rule that makes it very difficult to find optimal health, people who have sinus and allergy problems. I highly recommend working diligently to try to find remedies for everyday open mouth breathing due to a stuffed nose or sinuses. The filtering, heating, and moistening that is done through the nose purifies the air and readies it for use in our respiratory system and bloodstream. Breathing consistently through the mouth is not as healthy as breathing through the nose.

LifeBreath can be done lying, seated, or standing, but a full breath session is most often done lying comfortably, with knees either bent or straight. Knees can be propped up and supported with a pillow. The head is usually in a neutral position, not tipped forward. The tilting forward of the head can restrict the throat region. Occasionally we prop the neck, chest or diaphragm upward to help open an area if there is a lot of restriction. The floor should support arms and legs.

(Using a regular massage table to breathe can be awkward because your arms need to be supported and you need to be able to move around.)

When It's Done

> *"I love to breathe with my children."* —CC

> *"I breathe before I meditate and it really helps me go so much deeper."* —BN

> *"I breathe religiously every morning and every night. I have a very busy life and it helps me prioritize and relax into life. I find it helps me make better business decisions and simply better life decisions. When you have four kids, run a business and have fifteen employees, how could you get along without breath and not go crazy?"* —SC

> *"When I'm stressed – I breathe"* —BF

> *"I love to breathe in a group. I feel so connected and loved. "* —MJ

LifeBreath can be done just about anywhere by anyone. One of the miracles of this breathing modality is that it works for everyone who is willing and able to open up and breathe more fully. It can be done for just a few breaths length or it can be done in an all-out breath session that can last up to a few hours.

To incorporate breath into your everyday life, you must begin *tuning in to* your body and you must become *conscious of your breathing*.

Become aware of when you **don't** breathe, when you hold your breath and how it *feels*. When this happens, it's a sign that *"something's up."* It can be a pattern that you have picked up through habitual non-breathing. It can also be due to discomfort (PEMS). We have learned that we hold our breath when we are in physical and emotional pain or when we are uncomfortable, but sometimes we even hold our breath when we're thinking too hard! We stop breathing when we feel overwhelmed. It is a coping tool associated with when we were warriors in the flight or fight mode; however, we are often ready to cope with a lot more than we do.

So, what is one to do? BREATHE! Ask yourself WHY you are not breathing. Habit? Discomfort? Emotionally overbearing situation? Then Breathe! Take a few deep belly breaths that roll up to the heart and sigh outward. Allow yourself to confront the very reason that you are not breathing. *These are all symptoms that lead us to understand that it is time to do a LifeBreath session.*

Remember:
One of our most important goals is to
become a habitual full and relaxed breather.

I recommend beginning your day with LifeBreath by staying in bed for an extra five to ten minutes to breathe. It will make your whole day begin more centered, clear, and energized. Ending your day and beginning your sleep-time with Breath will allow you to create an appreciation for the past day and a sense of letting go. It will also help start your sleep more centered and relaxed. If you have difficulty sleeping throughout the night, LifeBreath is a great tool to either help you fall back asleep or use the wakeful time for some of your homework for *Life School*.

Through performing an actual full LifeBreath session during some part of your day you can accelerate your physical, emotional, mental, and spiritual **attitude** and **latitude**. When I first began LifeBreath, I did a forty-five minute session every day for almost two years. It changed my life and many others have benefited from the same kind of regiment. If you do not have the time in your life to fit in a daily session, then Breathe as often as possible and as often as feels right to you. It all depends on how quickly you want to feel better and feel your best.

A five, ten, or even fifteen-minute session can be very beneficial too. A few minutes can truly enhance your day and can be used to prepare for many of our life's tasks, such as meditation, a nap, physical exercise, a meeting, a confrontation, getting your head cleared, or anything else you'd like to focus on. Any time you feel tired, upset, sluggish, off-kilter, or out of sorts, stop what you're doing and spend some time practicing LifeBreath. Any time you want to feel "ON," I can assure you, it will work to re-center, revitalize, and energize you.

A beneficial formula looks like this…

1. Breathe five - ten minutes in the a.m. when you wake
2. Breathe five - ten minutes in the p.m. to go to sleep by
3. Breathe at least 10 – 15 minutes some time throughout the day
   - Be conscious of holding your breath and **don't** …just breathe!
   - Become a habitual full, diaphragmatic, relaxed nostril breather
     (Use the Nine Keys to Healthy Normal Breathing as a guide)
4. Do a full LifeBreath session as often as you can or as often as feels right.
5. This can be achieved through:
   - A guided facilitated session
   - A guided group session
   - The guided LifeBreath audio tape/CD

Remember: As you breathe, do not make your breath right or wrong, only more and more effective and open.

Life and Breath are a journey.
Allow yourself to be open and expand.

Where It's Done

> *"I am an avid (scuba) diver. I've done incredible sessions in the water while breathing through a snorkel. It was so cool."*
> —MM

> *"I love to breathe in nature. I'll go for a hike, lay down on top of a mountain and just breathe in the beauty. I always have awesome sessions up there."* —TW

> *"I do little mini-breath sessions in my car in traffic. It helps me cope…"* —SM

> *"Sometimes I breathe at work. It's very stressful. I wish my boss would breathe."* —BB

LifeBreath can be done just about anywhere, but certain environments will enhance your sessions. Finding a safe, disturbance-free area is best. We have our *"breathroom"* in our home. It's a spare bedroom that has become a sacred space for us. We have set it up for our family and our clients to create the best results possible. A comfortable lying space, futon or mat is great.

I've done sessions with people on the ground, on chairs, in the woods, on boats, in water, even in airplanes. Blankets, tissues, water, and music are all important, but not essential. Having a bathroom close by is also a benefit. *LifeBreath can work a little like herbal tea, flushing out the toxins in any way possible.*

What May Happen During A LifeBreath Session

*Every LifeBreath session is different and each session changes as **you** change. Experiences may range from being very physical to emotional and psycho-spiritual.*

<u>Physically</u>

When you begin the first few minutes of breathing, you may feel a little light headed and/or experience a dry mouth. This almost always goes away. Very rarely, the dry mouth or feeling light headed may stay throughout the session, but it's quite tolerable, especially weighing it against all the benefits.

You may get very cold, very hot, or both, at different times throughout the session. The cold can be bone chilling and you may begin to shiver. The cold is not from an external, environmental chill – it is from doing this type of energy work. Having blankets on hand is helpful, but does not always treat the cold. Becoming hot and sweaty is common. This can be due to the detoxification process. The chill or heat is nothing more than your physical body working through the contracted energy in the PEMS realms.

Vibrating, tingling, or humming is also a common occurrence. It usually starts in the hands, feet, and jaw and can work towards the core of the body. When you tingle, you are feeling your own life energy. It can be a light sense of vibration or it can become very intense. Over time, the intensity wanes and the flow of energy becomes easy and extremely pleasurable.

This feeling of vibration, heat, buzzing, or intense energy can occur where there is old physical or emotional trauma. For instance, if you have an old shoulder injury, the chi that is flowing through your body may work its way into the shoulder. It acts like a "roto-rooter" and begins to bring life energy back to the blocked area. This vibration may be interpreted as what we call "pain," but it is actually just intense energy. Many people have claimed to have miraculous results through breath with physical ailments and chronic pain.

You may feel your chakras stimulated, along with the emotions they carry. Your pubic area, belly, diaphragm, heart, or throat may buzz or swirl, feeling heavy, tight, or energized. If the energy feels heavy or stuck, you may actually feel it let go. This process may take place in the matter of just a few breaths or over the course of a few sessions.

The energy and vibration can become very intense. You may feel a bearing down on the muscles, making the muscles feel tight. The medical field calls this tightness tetany and it is due, in part, to hyperventilating. *Hyperventilation, however, can not occur if our breathing is relaxed and calm.* Most of your energy is being routed towards the torso throughout a breath session and the tetany occurs where the energy is being drawn away from our extremities, mouth, and jaw. There is also a balance in the body that "normal" breathing brings, the ph balance, along with other chemical reactions, are thrown off and through this disruption, tetany may occur.

Emotionally, tetany occurs when people *"hold on to old stuff."* There is usually some kind of resistance against letting go, change, or healing. A release in emotional energy almost always rids the body of tetany completely and immediately. It's an amazing thing to watch. When the emotional release occurs, the tetany can go away instantly, in seconds. If the emotions become too intense, simply slowing the breath down and relaxing the breath will bring down the feelings and allow for slower release. Quick shallow breaths are an excellent way to ride the waves of intensity towards resolution.

During a Breath session, a breather may perceive that the breath is what is making them feel out of sorts, when actually it's the contracted, unresolved energy that is the culprit. The best way to resolve the difficulty is to continue to breathe. This allows the breather to get to the other side of the emotion. When facilitating a session for someone like this, I often say…

> ***Sometimes you have to swim through the muck to get to the rainbow that is waiting on the other side.***

There may be one more reason for tetany or other physical discomfort during a session. I believe we are vessels filled with energy and spirit. During a breath session this vessel may be filled with more energy/spirit than ever before, so the physical feelings are the discomfort of being so extremely charged and full. It's like a hose that usually carries five gallons of water and then suddenly you put in twenty gallons. It must expand in order to handle the new volume. That's what happens during an intense breath session; the volume is turned up. I believe it is divine healing power within us.

Some good news:

Your vessel gets to keep that higher volume of energy/spirit after the session. You begin living at a new vibration of light. People often communicate that they felt overwhelmed, but overwhelmed with love, spirit, and goodness.

However, if you do not continue to feed this new energy and you go back to your old ways, (depleting your chi), you can lose it.

This breathwork merges the inner and outer breath of the universe and you get to experience divine energy in the physical body. *Let's face it, that can be overwhelming.* This work is ninety-nine percent pleasurable and only one percent not. The one percent is about holding on to old negativity and pain and being fearful about coming out of your comfort/safety zone. Many sensations can be physically felt like fear, sadness, and grief. Pain is the process of being freed from those emotions. Once this sensation quickly passes, you get to experience love, joy, divine energy, and bliss.

You are in charge of your session. People often move around or even tone (make sound). Movement and toning are tools that can be used to help move energy, but should not be used to avoid breathing. Movement and toning are practices used with breath, but can also be used separately as transformation tools.

On a few occasions, during the detoxification process, I have actually smelled anesthesia, alcohol, pot, tobacco, and fumes. One client of mine had done some work in a float tank and she swallowed some of the salt water. It was not a pleasant experience and it occurred years prior to her first breath session. She, unknowingly, carried some fear around with her about the event. During her first few breath sessions, she tasted the salt water while she was detoxifying and integrating the experience.

I have another client who welds for a living in huge ships, deep in the hulls where there is poor ventilation. All day long, year after year, he is poisoned with the fumes. Each time he breathes, his skin literally crawls with the toxins. He has to breathe with a towel under him because he profusely sweats and he smells like fumes. The sessions are quite powerful and detoxifying.

It is not uncommon for people to yawn or cough during a session. A yawn helps move energy and is not a bad thing in the least. Coughing opens the throat and compassion centers and can assist in purging restricted energy. The cough is literally coughing up our constricted emotions. Laughing, yelling, yawning, screaming, sighing, giggling, and gasping are all emotionally releasing and they also help move energy.

Phasing out, or stopping one's breathing, is fairly common. It can be a result of one of two things. First, phasing out can be a way of avoiding and continuing to push down an emotion. I encourage people to breathe when they temporarily stop. Have you ever seen someone who held his or her breath a long time because an emotion was trying to come up? Or have you been with a child who held their breath in pain or anger? You want to tell that person…*breathe, breathe, breathe*. But they are unable to until they are ready to release.

The other condition where people phase out is when they are experiencing **rapture**. *They are going, going, GONE* !! They have left this plane for another and it's a wonderful, incredible phenomenon. Until you have experienced this, it is very difficult to explain. Sometimes people remember where they have been and what they have seen. However, some people don't remember. Either way, they feel a sense of love and connection that is beyond words.

Holly had a multitude of physical ailments she suffered through over the last twenty years of her life. She was overweight, stressed, diabetic, and had difficulty moving and breathing. Her heart was weak and she was beginning to give up on life. Holly came to me through a recommendation by her physician and therapist. The most difficult part of the session was finding a comfortable position for her to breathe in. Once we got her comfortable, we eased into her breathing pattern.

Amazingly, she was amazingly able to fully breathe into all parts of her wave – belly, diaphragm, and chest. During her session she felt many physical sensations from tingling to heaviness to tension and then finally an easiness.

We talked a great deal afterwards about how the physical body is so interconnected with the mental and emotional bodies. She agreed to breathe daily and to begin reading some holistic books I recommended. She said she felt a little lighter and a quite a bit better.

The next week, we did a second session. Holly was quite open to the breath this time. She had decided that she truly WANTED to LIVE, especially for her grandson who she often cared for. She was scheduled for surgery for her heart and was determined to either avoid the surgery totally or at least go into the surgery with a healthier body and a new attitude.

Her session was very powerful. She felt just about every physical thing you could possibly experience. She was very excited over the fact that she was so able to fully feel for the first time in many years.

We continued a few more private sessions, but then Holly felt able to attend a group session. She LOVED the energy there. She felt she made some new wonderful friends. Holly began to do things with her new found friends that she never thought possible. Her body was getting healthier. People were asking her to take walks, go shopping, and attend some of our daylong workshops. Holly was transforming.

Holly is still on an upward spiral. She is feeling more alive and healthier than ever before. She spends energetic quality time with her grandson and she is off many of her medications. She continues to grow, become healthier and now she's even helping other people on their path towards a healthier, and happier life.

Mentally

"Just a single thought is capable of changing the breathing pattern." ——Ilse Middendorf

"Breathing in, I calm my body and mind. Breathing out, I smile. Dwelling in the present moment, I know this is the only moment." ——Thich Nhat Hanh

"To our ordinary consciousness, breathing only serves to maintain our body. But if we go beyond our mind, breathing can open up a completely new foundation for our life." ——Ilsa Middendorf

LifeBreath sessions are filled with different waves, like a roller coaster ride of events. Throughout the session you may or may not be aware of your surroundings or your physical body. You can experience altered states of consciousness, much like dreaming.

If you are a very worrisome, nervous person, your anxiety can hinder your ability to let go and be present to whatever is happening. I recommend that people relax into their breathing and just let what ever comes, come. Worriers and busy-minded people can receive great results from the session once they let go a little. This occurs once the person trusts the Breath, themselves, the facilitator, and the transformational process. *It's magical.*

A sense of mental clarity can occur during and after a session that may be unprecedented. I have heard many accounts, in addition to my own experiences, where people who have meditated all their lives have achieved higher states of consciousness in one Breath session than in all the years of meditating; of course, this is not at all to undermine the importance of meditation.

When a Breath session becomes physically and emotionally difficult, it is important to stay focused. Oftentimes people experience things outside of their comfort zone. The session can be intensely physical (hot, cold, tingling, muscle tension, muscle tremors, hypersensitive areas, nausea due to purging, light headedness). It can be mentally and/or emotionally laborious too, but by staying focused, you can push through limitations and contracted energy and experience deep relaxation, powerful insights, visions, colors, guides, angels, and lights. It can be a sensual, joyful, mystical experience and a spiritual rebirth.

Susan couldn't "get into" Breathing for many years. Every time she Breathed her mind would wander and she would grow very nervous. She would only breathe for a few minutes and then quit. She would try once every few years to breathe, but she felt unsuccessful and very anxious. Her mind was kept busy by shutting down her emotions. Her breath was extremely shallow and we both knew she would eventually have to deal with her sexual abuse as a child. She was not yet ready.

Susan finally went to counseling and became more open to really committing to healing and actually doing a full session. Her first "real" session was wonderful! Her mind was more relaxed and because of the work she was doing with her therapist, she was able to stay with the whole session. We went further in that one session (because of her commitment and where her mind/emotions were) than all the other sessions combined.

After the session, Susan shared that her mind did not wander. Even though she came face to face with her nightmare, she was able to stay focused and breathe through it. She cried a lot, but it was truly releasing. She is doing wonderful work around forgiveness, healing, and finding new ways of expressing herself. Her mind is clearer and she is breathing more fully than ever before.

Emotionally

> *"Emotional and physical states can be altered by changing the breathing pattern."* —Weilhelm Reich

We now understand that the Physical, Emotional, Mental, and Spiritual systems are so interconnected that there is no way to actually separate them. As we breathe in large amounts of chi during a LifeBreath session, emotions that are hidden, locked and contracted deep in our being often come out of hiding. So much of our daily energy is robbed from holding onto those old emotions and it is a wonderful and glorious day when they surface. When they do come to the surface we can acknowledge, fully deal with, and resolve the emotions involved. All things naturally surface in layers. *If it all came out at one time, we'd probably implode!*

So, during a session we often feel emotions. *YAY!* What a place to honor yourself! What a safe haven to do our lifework.

Laughter, sorrow, giggles, sadness, grief, joy, and all the love and fear associated with life can be felt. It's a joyous occasion when someone cries. It's a joyous occasion when someone feels.

Sometimes we can remember an old experience that brought us pain and continues to bring us pain because we have not resolved it yet. Remembering a past experience is much less important than the feelings that it evokes. Once the feelings have been acknowledged, one can choose to live in the past or live in the moment. I have had people tell me that they felt more emotion during a Breath session than they had all their lives. One man told me he had not cried in his adult life until LifeBreath. During his session he wept and wept. Since then, he has cried tears of sorrow and joy. He says LifeBreath has brought him a deep sense of compassion, love, and forgiveness.

Part of the magic of this Breath is that people only feel what they are ready to feel. There is a natural barometer inside each of us that knows what you are ready to handle.

While circulating energy throughout the body, whatever emotion or sensation most needs healing at that moment stands out and asks for our attention. The conscious and unconscious unite which brings spirit into the body. It balances our energy and "highlights" the areas where resistance can be embraced. Without consciously being aware, we move towards wholeness and healing.

Many holistic healing modalities and other breathwork has us examine our "old stuff." For LifeBreath purposes, we feel this is not always necessary. The Breath is THAT powerful.

There are two other miracles that I have witnessed over and over again:

1. **An emotion that is twenty years old and twenty pounds heavy can have a huge layer removed (let go of) in just one session.**

2. **Grief, sadness, and old pain are registered in the body as just that – grief, sadness, and old pain. Where it comes from does not necessary matter. You don't have to remember the details in order to let go of the emotion!**

Some people will only participate in one facilitated Breath session. Some will come for the rest of their lives *to be Breathed*. Everyone is different with individual special needs. I used to become frustrated or unsure of the effectiveness of a session if someone did not return for more Breathwork. but I eventually found my worry unwarranted. After a few years of teaching LifeBreath, people who came to just one session would cross my path and tell me how it changed their lives and that they'll never forget what it did for them. I finally figured out that one session (or two or whatever) was all they were ready, willing, and able to do at that time. Each session and every experience is just right for them.

I had one woman follow my car into my driveway at one o'clock in the morning when I was returning home from teaching a seminar. She told me that she had wanted to call me many times, but was afraid to let me know how deeply she was affected from her session. She said she was completely cured of shingles and the blindness that was setting in from the side effects of the illness. After that, she also lost a lot of weight and stopped smoking. To his date, she has still only done two sessions, but is a great proponent of our work.

> *"Having passed through such a trauma and such subsequent healing, the individual will release the contracted energy, thus feeling immediately better, while circumventing any long-term problems. Furthermore, the event will have opened the person to a host of expanded, positive possibilities – he or she may well be stronger, wiser, healthier, or more loving. Indeed, the very intensity of the negative experience, with its great charge of excited energy, will determine just how positive the outcome can be."*
> —Michael Sky, Breathing

Tracy came to a group Breath session at the health club where she worked out. During her first session she became choked up in her throat. Her throat lifted and she was unable to get a comfortable Breath up through her chest. I held her in my arms and she began to relax and was able to gently breathe. We talked for a little while and we set up a private session for a few days later.

Tracy shared her story. She was on the verge of a nervous breakdown. She was having severe panic attacks and was close to being committed to a hospital, and they would take away her infant child.

Needless to say, she really needed to breathe. Her session was miraculous. She had every physical and emotional experience I had ever seen. She laughed, cried, grieved, ranted, raved, and even went out into altered states of consciousness many times. Her session was about two and a half hours long. Because of my trust, faith, and knowledge of the Breath, I knew she was in the middle of a miracle.

We did two more consecutive sessions throughout that week. She was an extremely brave and committed soul, and all the work paid off. She went to counseling with her husband, did not have to be hospitalized, did not lose her child, and has since since been studying all kinds of healing holistic practices. The last time I saw Tracy she no longer had panic attacks and she was able to travel,(her attacks happened at red lights and bridges, deeming it almost impossible to go anywhere. She had some attacks with her infant in the car and it was very scary for her and all of her loved ones). Tracy told me that she continues to use the Breath for maintenance, during stressful times and as a type of meditation that helps balance and calm her.

Sally came to do a Breath session because she felt that she needed to learn to relax. Her life was falling apart, she thought, because she didn't know how to manage stress. She was athletic up to her teen years, but after a car accident, she has had chronic pain and has gained almost one hundred pounds. Her job is stagnant and unrewarding. Both of her parents had passed over, and she has little memory of her childhood, only that her father was an abusive alcoholic and her mother was not attentive or supportive. She was married for a short time to an alcoholic and has had "crazy" relationships since, often having sexual affairs with married men. Her physical ailments included sleeplessness, hair loss, diabetes, heart disease, spinal disfunction, chronic pain, obesity, high blood pressure and binging. She said that she was basically a happy person who didn't mind being alone, but when we talked more in depth she admitted she was really quite depressed. She put on a good facade using laughter and a hard external shell, but inside she was dying and her illnesses were speaking loud and clear.

Sally's first LifeBreath session was quite remarkable. She realized that she held a lot of anger in her physical body. During her session, she wept a lot and afterwards she had a few days of decreased physical pain. I had her Breathe daily for ten minutes in the morning and ten minutes in the evening to help relax and integrate her first experience.

Sally's second session was much more intense. Her rage against her father and mother was finally being vocalized and expressed. She said that she had no idea how much hatred she carried around her father and how it affected her today. However, she was not ready to completely forgive him yet. She felt all her problems stemmed from her dad's abusive behavior and it was HIS FAULT she was fat, in pain and depressed. We also discussed how Sally's relationships with men who were unattainable was one way for her to punish herself again and again.

We talked about how, by NOT forgiving her parents, she was allowing them to hurt her over and over and that SHE was the one punishing herself now, not them. Sally intellectually understood this concept, but she said, " I don't know how I can ever forgive them. I still feel as though they ruined my life." So, we set an appointment for another Breath session and we agreed it would be beneficial for her to read "The Courage to Heal."

Two weeks later a miracle occurred during her breath session. Sally explained it this way:

"I was breathing away and all of a sudden I saw a vision of myself as a child. I was actually happy and I was playing and kind of humming. My mom came along and gently grabbed one of my hands and my father gently grabbed the other. We walked along a country road, just the three of us, silently, and then we began to hum together. I just can't really explain it, but this overall sense of love between us three came upon me and I knew that everything was going to be all right. I felt my heart open like never before and I began to weep tears of gratitude and forgiveness. At the end of our walk, we just kind of disappeared into the end of the road like the end of a good movie where everyone lived happily ever after.

Since that breath session, Sally has lost weight, gained confidence and has begun to think much more positively. She is exercising because her pain has greatly diminished and her doctor told her if she continues on this path she could very possibly go off all her diabetes and heart medicine.

We talked the other day and she has been reading some wonderful books. She's beginning to understand that she is responsible for her view in life and for co-creating her destiny. But most remarkably, she is beginning to understand that her past has had wonderful spiritual life lessons, and that through forgiveness she has begun to love herself and others again.

<u>S</u>piritually

> "I add my breath to your breath
> That our days may be long on the Earth
> That the days of our people may be long
> That we may be one person."
> —Ancient Keres Song,
> translated by Paula Gunn Alan

Spirituality is such a personal part of LifeBreath because it is expressed and felt in so many loving ways.

People have sensed the presence of spirit while Breathing. Experiences range from feeling the "touch of God" to feeling the presence of a loved one, or feeling more at peace with themselves. *"The oneness and love of all"* is the way one breather explained the feeling.

Breathing in and out is profoundly spiritual unto itself. The energy that flows inward is, in itself, spirit and chi. It is what the ancient people expressed when they named breath and spirit as one. The feeling of vibration is essentially the feeling of *spirit* and our physical body merging.

> *"The Latin word for breath is spiritus. Allow your breath to flow through you as a sense of spirit flows through your body."* —Jerry Braza, MD.

> *"The purpose of conscious breathing is not primarily the movement of air, but the movement of energy. If you do a relaxed, connected breathing cycle for a few minutes, you will experience dynamic energy flows within your body. These energy flows are the merging of spirit and matter."*
> —Leonard Orr, <u>Rebirthing</u>

Altered states of consciousness can be attained through Breathing. It is not uncommon to be able to discern between the physical body and the spirit during a LifeBreath session. People can remember being "out" somewhere, but they may not remember where. However, they often feel heightened awareness, a sense of peace and a clearer vision of their life purpose. Sometimes people are "out there" and remember quite precisely where they have been and who they have shared time with, along with receiving important messages and intuitive awareness.

Specifically regarding intuition, LifeBreath can profoundly help people to *tap into* higher guidance. Whatever your beliefs are about intuition and spiritual guidance, people have finished sessions with a true sense of connection and spiritual transformation.

Breathwork has allowed me the grace to live a more spiritual life. I see more clearly, I love more deeply and I feel more connected to people and the universe than I ever thought possible. I sense, very profoundly, what I have always believed in; God and a very close connection to my spirit. This is MY personal experience. YOU will have your own interpretation of your experience, but most people have at least reported a heightened sense of spirituality.

> *Some of the more spiritual sessions I have witnessed were with my brother, Mark. His first session involved revisiting my father's death. It was actually quite humorous at first. He saw my father's soul leave his body and heard my father (in a kind of Jackie Gleason funny way) say, "uh oh, here I go." At first, Mark laughed, but then he cried. We both figured out it was a way of grieving my dad, but the comedy was also very apropos.*

After a Session

Once a session is over, it's not really always over. You have brought in large quantities of chi and have united with the energy of spirit. It doesn't just go away. You have begun unrestricting the flow of life energy. You have begun your transformation process using LifeBreath.

It can take some time to get back on your feet immediately following a session. I recommend scheduling plenty of time to recuperate. You may feel a little light headed, tired, exhausted, energized, hungry, starving, thirsty, etc., as a result of your experience with heightened senses.

Sometimes the emotions that are brought up during a session may linger throughout a period of time afterwards. You may feel so wonderful that your feet don't touch the ground for a few days. You may feel a little "yukky" because you "unstuffed your stuffed stuff" and need time to process. Remember, we often have to swim through a little of that mucky stuff to get to the good stuff in life (the other side of the rainbow). It is time for reflection and self-care. Another session may be needed sooner rather than later to help you *through* an emotion that has surfaced but has not been fully resolved and integrated. It can take some time to feel somewhat normal. *Hopefully, if normal didn't feel so great, you'll never feel normal again, only better and better.*

It's important to drink lots of water, eat healthy, and care for your soul.

Teresa called me after her first session at around 11:00 p.m. and wanted to know what the heck was going on... she couldn't sleep. She said she was so energized and wired that there was no way she would sleep all night. I told her to just surrender to it, enjoy it, and perhaps try to spend some time in reflection. She had experienced a very powerful session that afternoon and it opened many channels of emotional and physical energy.

Teresa did many more sessions, but her family was concerned because she would react afterwards, with strong mood swings. Her husband called me, in concern, wanting to know just what it was we were doing and how it works. I explained and also added that if he thought Teresa would benefit from counseling, by all means, the two of them could decide.

After a little time of struggle, Teresa's life began to open up. Her husband was seeing positive transformation in her. In fact, Teresa began feeling better about herself and specifically her body. Her husband was VERY pleased about her new found sexuality. He began encouraging her to go to group (and eventually the LifeBreath Personal Power and Growth Course) rather than discouraging her. I think their sex life is even better now than when they were newlyweds.

Good job working through the "after the session stuff!"

LifeBreath as a Tool to Meet the Needs of Special Populations

Respiratory Disease, Pain or Trauma

People who have respiratory disease often benefit more by being seated up when doing LifeBreath. It allows for less pressure on the chest and assists them to get a fuller breath. People with chronic pain, especially back pain, may need to be propped up or lay on their side. Likewise, anyone who has been traumatized, especially in a lying position, may benefit from breathing seated up as they may feel less vulnerable and more comfortable.

Pregnant Woman

Pregnant women need to find the most comfortable position for them and often need to move around more.

Infants and Children

Infants are facilitated on your chest. Just Breathe with them. Small, young children can be Breathed on your chest or by "spooning" them (placing their back to your chest). Older children may be instructed. Children usually only need to practice LifeBreath in very short doses because they do not have the deeply implanted restrictions that adults carry and they don't have as many serious "issues" to deal with.

Counseling and Psychotherapy

LifeBreath is a powerful tool in conjunction with counseling and psychotherapy. Many of the clients I see are simultaneously seeking professional counseling and therapy. Where these modalities work with the mind and emotions, LifeBreath assists on a physical cellular level and a spiritual level too. It's a perfect marriage for positive change.

Safe for Anyone

We can create a safe, comfortable space for just about anyone who wants to try the LifeBreath Technique. It is safe to adapt the Breath by teaching it through the nose (if necessary), doing it in any position, focusing it to go anywhere in the body that we deem important, or we can create any changes that help the Breather become more agile and fluent in Breathwork.

One of the most profound Breath sessions I facilitated years ago was with a very small infant. My partner was busy facilitating Lily's parents. Her mother was white and her father was black. They were going through horrific family problems because of the interracial marriage. Lily was severely mentally retarded with a plethora of health problems. Her grandparents were not communicating with her parents and the war was wreaking havoc in everyone's life. Little Lily was the only thing they all had in common. The doctors believed she was inevitably going to die before she turned three as a result of all her illnesses. Wasn't there any way these people could get along?

I took Lily to my chest while lying down with her. I began to Breathe with her, heart to heart. She was unable to lift her head so I just laid it on my shoulder. I breathed into my belly and into my heart. I played beautiful heart music and we breathed together for quite some time. She was completely relaxed and loving the energy. Suddenly, she lifted her head, looked straight into my eyes and said with her eyes, "It's all ok. Yes, I am going to die, but my short time here is to teach my family love."

Wow, I have to tell you... I lost it. I cried and cried and felt as though I had felt her special love. It made me believe in miracles. It made me know that we just don't understand so many things in life. Through this child, I got to experience the most unconditional love of my life.

LifeBreath Breathing Analysis

Breathing analysis allows me to understand the breathing of an individual. Most importantly, it allows me to better help that person. I can take notice of the breathing pattern and decide how to best serve this person, through modifying their breathing and using complimentary LifeBreath tools.

As the breath is executed, I look for a full, relaxed circular breathing pattern that circulates through all parts of the breathing cycle, from the pubic bone to the mouth. Anywhere through the cycle that there are interruptions or disturbances, it tells me energy is being restricted.

I observe:

- The overall look and feeling of the breath
- Where the breath goes
- How much breath there is
- Is it equal in all areas?
- Where are there hesitations or restrictions?
- The speed of the breath
- The relationship between the inhale and the exhale
- How the breath comes into each area and in what order

Also see "Common Breathing Restrictions for Everyday Life"

**As people transform, their breath changes
and, as their breath changes, people transform.**

What is the Overall Look and Feeling of the Breath?

As I have indicated before, the inhale represents all the *good stuff* in life and the exhale represents our ability to let go and to surrender. Ultimately, this is what I look at during breathing analysis. A "perfect" breath looks different on each person. Our breath is like a fingerprint, it is ours and it is completely unique. As a LifeBreath facilitator, I work with a person's particular pattern and help them go back to the *baby's breath*, open their breathing, and create transformation.

It is good when the inhale is fairly large and robust, representing a good sense of peace, abundance, joy, and love (and how much of these things we are presently capable of receiving). When the exhale is relaxed and acts like a sigh, it means letting go is not too difficult and we do not hold on to the past or future too tightly.

The exhale tells us what we do with negativity. Do we hold on? Control? Manipulate? Or surrender and shift our paradigms easily?

I usually look at the breath and give it an adjective. I have found that the adjective corresponds with the breather's general sense about life.

I may name an inhale or exhale generally as:

- Flowing or restricted
- Relaxed or uptight
- Labored or easy
- Filled with struggle or easy
- Stressed or unstressed
- Restricted or open
- Natural or mechanical
- Rough or smooth
- Even or uneven
- Cautious or trusting
- Filled with fear or filled with love
- Hesitant or certain

These traits are directly associated with the person's general belief about life. If the inhale is difficult, they might believe that the *good stuff in life* is difficult to manifest. If the exhale is difficult, they usually have a hard time letting go and may hold onto old negative energy.

When the inhale is filled with struggle, the breather may have had experiences that have been perceived as hard. Depending on where the struggle lies, for example in the heart, I would associate the breath with a hurt heart. If the inhale is difficult, the breather may find it difficult to let love *in*. If the exhale is harder, it may be about *letting go* around the heart.

If the breath is unnatural, it usually means that the person has probably not breathed like this (full, open, circular, etc.) in a very long time, probably since childhood. Their lives have may have become disconnected and unnatural. When the inhale and exhale are drastically out of synch and very uneven, it can represent life being out of balance.

So, you see how it goes:

**The breath never lies. It tells the story of our life.
Our breath and our life are synonymous.**

Where Does the Breath Go? How Does the Breath Come Into and In What Order Does it Fill the Body?

I must take into account the speed, quality, and quantity of the Breath while watching where the air goes and in what order it fills the body.

I look to see if and when the breath goes to the lower belly (all the way down to the pubic bone), belly, diaphragm, lower and upper chest, and into the throat.

When and where the breath goes into the body is directly associated to our chakra system. When we do not breathe into a certain area in the body, this non-breathing can act like a painkiller, like anesthesia. We stop breathing there for a reason, as it probably hurts too much.

Here's what we can conclude about Breathing Analysis:

When there is no breath in the belly, we can see issues around security, survival, sexuality, family, worthiness, and self-image. The breather is afraid to feel and may be unwilling to change. It is not uncommon for people who have been abused or assaulted to shut down in the belly. There can be anger, fear, and a general sense of being unsafe and disconnected attributed to the shutting off of the belly breath.

Women especially have become non-belly breathers. I believe it is not a coincidence that women's ailments in the lower abdominal region are on the increase. Lower back pain, cancer, menstrual and menopause problems, and lower organ ailments are occurring on an epidemic scale. Many women I facilitate have very little, even no breath in this area. As they begin to bring life force back into the abdomen, the emotional and physical dis-ease is eased or altogether abandoned.

Little or no breath in the diaphragm often represents a loss of power and a holding on to fear. A person who does not breathe into the solar plexus can loose the ability to correctly assess situations and may be caught in a spiral of fear, pain, and judgement. This is a center that commonly holds restriction. Known as the fear belt, the fight or flight response, muscular tensions, and emotional trauma is held in the solar plexus. By releasing this restricted area and focusing the breath there, quantum leaps in our healing process may occur.

An overly active diaphragm, on the other hand, where the breath is dramatically larger there than anywhere else, often depicts a separation between heart and will. This is a person who has had to build a separate identity, perhaps because of an overbearing figure in their life.

It is in the heart where we hold the energy of love, harmony, compassion, forgiveness, trust, and hope. When the breath is restricted around the heart, we often have a dampened sense of feeling. We may have been wounded and hurt and now have difficulty giving and receiving love. Loss, grief, bitterness, and hate can restrict the heart. By restricting the heart, we also deny ourselves of greater amounts of joy, peace, and love. More common in men, perhaps because of the taboo around men showing their emotions, lack of heart breathing causes many physical problems too. When the heart is shut down, coronary dis-ease is prevalent, across the entire Physical, Emotional, Mental, and Spirittual systems. When the heart is overly active, it's as though the person is overcompensating for some kind of loss or grief. It's as though they're trying too hard.

The throat center represents creativity, expression, communication, and higher will. When this area is closed, the inhale and exhale sound and feel tense. In this world, many of us do not have full open expression. Throat center restriction represents our inability to fully express and connect to our higher will.

I have seen people whose breathing patterns shift all over the place. On one inhale the breath is big in the heart. The next breath is big in the belly. The next breath is reverse breathing, etc. etc. I call this "world war three" breathing. This represents the perception of life as hysterical, sporadic, turmoil-filled, and out of balance. Hysterical and sporadic breathing usually means that the person is unsure if they can handle it all and that they are overwhelmed by life's struggles. They also have lots of doubt around their own greatness and experience a lack of self confidence.

"Warrior Breath" is a belly-only breath. This person is usually very grounded, but has difficulty showing their heart and expressing themselves. There is little or no breath above the belly, so the diaphragm, heart, and throat are all shut down and not activated. This person may be very shut down emotionally.

Sometimes the breath comes into the body in reverse order. The breath enters the heart first and then the belly. This may be due to the breather living more in the heart and being less grounded.

There is a breathing pattern called "reverse breathing." This occurs when the belly is sucked inward during inhale and pushed outward during the exhale. Illness and dis-ease in the abdominal region or midsection of the body is commonly associated with this breath. Specifically, many cancer patients arrive at a LifeBreath session with reverse breathing. Many of the people who demonstrate this kind of breathing are generally very uptight. They may have sucked in their belly all their lives, and reteaching them abdominal breathing can be truly life altering, especially when he or she can get past their old physical and mental patterns. I take reverse breathing very seriously and work diligently to assist the breather in not only correcting the pattern, but understanding how the patterned showed up in the first place.

How Much Breath is There?
Is it Equal in All Areas?

I watch how much breath goes into each area, and how the areas relate to one another. For example, if there is a dominant, struggle-filled breath in the heart and little or no breath elsewhere, I surmise that there is lots of struggle in the heart and a shutting down of the emotions in the belly and diaphragm.

When there is almost no breath anywhere (!), I understand that this person is extremely cautious, really hesitant and most likely filled with a lot of fear. He or she is VERY careful about who and what they let in. They usually have low self-esteem with little or no sense of peace, joy, or love. They may find it very difficult to let go. I'll ask the person to take the absolute largest breath they can muster up, and to my amazement, there is almost no movement in the entire wave. The more severe this "non-breathing," the more fearful, cautious, and hesitant I know they are. Through lots of love and hard work, the non-breather can transform into a healthy, open, loving, fearless, breathing person.

When the exhale is very small, this person usually has difficulty letting go and holds on to the past with fear and over-concern about the future. This can cause bottling up of emotions and a general sense of being overwhelmed by life. As emotions are released, it takes perseverance, strength, bravery and true desire to transform. By changing and working through the different breathing patterns of LifeBreath, one can expedite this process and go through the changes very quickly.

When the exhale is forceful, the breather is blowing things away, pushing away their negativity and they are usually fearful of the past and/or future.

When the belly is huge and very little wave elsewhere, this person is usually overcompensating. The heart is shut down. The diaphragm can be restricted too.

When the inhale is overly large, he or she is outwardly confident, but inwardly working very hard, overcompensating on the outside, but filled with inward turmoil and struggle.

Where Are There Hesitations or Restrictions?

I watch for little hiccups or glitches in the breath, hesitations that are like restrictions.

When there is a pause or holding of the breath after an inhale, the breather is usually holding on to old grief, old pain, negativity, and/or judgement. When the pause is after the exhale, this breather is not ready to fully accept joy and love into their life.

Hesitation around the belly, diaphragm, heart, or throat represents a "holding on to" of some sort on the exhale. And, if the hesitation is on the inhale, it represents a feeling of not being able to receive *"more of"* or a feeling of unworthiness.

How Fast or Slow Does the Inhale and Exhale Come In?

When the inhale is very fast and restricted, there may be a false sense that life is hard and there is struggle and difficulty. During this phase of a Breath session, there may be a lot of integration going on. Rapid breathing has great transformational properties. If it is restricted, we work together to get through this and work towards openness in the breath. If the lips are pursed on the inhale, like sucking out of a straw, and the breath is fast, even more struggle abounds. Pursed lips on the inhale also correlates to controlling the amount of divine energy that comes into the body. This can represent our unworthiness paradigm. If the lips are pursed and the inhale is slow, this represents the paradigm that there is a perceived need to be in control over how much *good* we can or should receive.

When the exhale is very fast and restricted, it usually represents pushing away negativity or the pushing down of an emotion that is being brought up. Once again, if it is fast and unrestricted, great leaps in *letting go* can occur. If it is restricted and pushed out, the more forceful the push, the more the breather pushes away acceptance in life. When the lips are pursed on the exhale, you really get to see how the breather literally blows away and controls negativity, surrender and acceptance. The exhale can also be done very slowly and restricted, which, again, represents control and the inability to let go.

In General

A "perfect breath" is different for each person. Your breathing will continuously change. There is no right or wrong, the breath just tells your story. Each breathing pattern is useful to assist us in reaching the next step forward in our transformational process.

**Allow your breathing to unfold and
watch how your life changes.**

**We are literally accessing divine energy
when we breathe.
Let's surrender to its power.**

I met Donna at a wonderful place called Camp Sunshine. It's a center that brings people from all over the country, without charge, to enjoy the beauty of Maine, spend time with friends and family and see doctors and counselors for particular illnesses, mainly cancer. Donna's husband was killed in N.Y. in the 9-11 attack and at Camp Sunshine for a special retreat.

I was teaching a class where we usually practice about forty-five minutes of chi kung and then a few minutes of LifeBreath. I explain the importance of breathing and how they can use it as a coping tool and to help them physically, emotionally, and psycho-spiritually. I invited anyone who wanted to stay afterwards to get a breathing analysis.

Donna's breath was quite fragmented and filled with some struggle. I explained to her that I was seeing a separation between her heart and her will. She didn't really know what I meant so I used this example. "It's as though you are a waitress or work as a teller, but you truly aspire to be a dancer. I can see your desire and I can see your disappointment and frustration." She and her friends began to laugh. Donna was working as a convenience store cashier, but she dreamed to be a dancer. I lucked out on my illustration, but Donna really got it. And wow, was she a believer.

Bobby came to a group session at our local hospital in Florida where I teach classes in Chi Kung. He stayed for a breathing analysis. He had a very nice open breath that started in his belly and beautifully flowed into his heart, but I saw some struggle in his upper chest. He had attended a few classes and he was having wonderful results. I went to Bobby's shoulders and back and touched a few points. He said they were quie painful, so I told him what I saw. "Your breath is very nice, beautiful, and flowing. It goes everywhere and that's great. I imagine you are a grounded, beautiful, loving person, but I see some struggle in your heart, upper back, and shoulders. Now, I could be wrong, but perhaps you carry a lot of weight in your heart and especially your shoulders. Are there a lot of people you carry? Are you weighted down? Has your heart been heavy?" Bobby was taken back that his breath could REVEAL all that and admitted it was right on the money. I heard him talking to someone afterwards and he was laughing about the fact that he had so many things on the burner and really was overwhelmed by it all. He owns a very large corporation with lots of "heavy" people around him.

I heard him say afterwards as he laughed, "How the heck does she know all that?"

It's all in the breath.

Transformational Tools Used During a LifeBreath Session

The Breath

We must never lose sight of the power of the breath itself. Without any of the tools that we use for assistance during a Breath session, the LifeBreath Technique is undoubtedly the most powerful tool unto itself.

We must never forget the breath's power and we must learn to trust in it.

Setting an Intention

What you focus on in life is what you attract. We are the creators of our destiny and this is true of a Breath session as well. I always ask people, *"If you could create a miracle in your session, what would it be?"* Most people make statments of intentions such as peace, love, happiness, clarity, abundance, inner strength, spiritual connection, and joy.

I recommend NOT focusing on, for example, weight loss, getting rid of something, or NOT having a particular feeling anymore. Again, what we focus on is what we receive, and if we focus on what we DON'T want, we will, often unknowingly, attract it. If I tell you NOT to think of a pink spotted elephant, you'll probably think of a pink spotted elephant, *get it?* This is, in part, why diets often do not work. If someone tells me I can't have chocolate any more, what do you think I crave? But, if I see myself as healthy and self-empowered, chocolate is not necessarily on my mind.

The miracles that are created through LifeBreath are simply just that — miracles. People have permanently transformed their lives in just one session. Sound too good to be true? *I challenge you. Try it!*

Music

The media is said to control our minds, but music controls our hearts. The music I play during a session can play an important, but not critical, part in the session. Very powerful sessions have happened on tops of mountains or floating on a lake where no music is available, but I use music to assist in opening hearts, as well as getting in touch with our innermost feelings.

Almost any kind of music can be used. Personally, I like strong music to begin a session so that powerful work levels can be achieved. During group sessions I find strong drumming music to be especially good. However, some individuals need softer, more subtle music to assist them in opening up. About midway through the session, I like heart music (flowing and loving), still fairly strong, and during the latter part, soft flowing heart music works best.

It is important that any of the aids to a Breath session… music, touch, movement, etc., are not confused or used to take away from the Breath's power. People can get caught up in these aids and if used improperly, they can distract from the Breath.

The music touches people's hearts in a profound way. Linda had a change of heart through the music we played during her session.

"When I heard the music at the end of the session, I just started bawling. I couldn't even help it. I don't know what it was. It was not at all bad, it was uplifting and I cried tears of joy. It was like the music was part of my heart. It was so powerful – it was wonderful."

Instruction During the Session

It's very helpful for the breather to receive instruction throughout the session to create the most pleasurable and transformational experience in the long run. A facilitator can help the breather learn how to tone, move into different positions or teach different variations of the breath. I may istruct someone to breathe a little faster, slower, breathe a little more here, or a little more there.

Body Mapping and Touch Points

There are many different modalities of energy work that have been used in cultures throughout the world for literally thousands of years. Information about chakra and meridians were depicted in history well over three thousands year ago. Body mapping correlates to the energy in the different chakras, meridians, pressure points and universal yin/yang concept around polarity. While studying at the Cosmic Breath Institute, body mapping was first introduced to me. It is very useful to help release and balance energy by touching points that loosely correlate to accupuncture points, as well as chakra points.

The left side of the body is our yin side – feminine, receptive, and negatively polarized. The right side of the body is our yang side – masculine, expressive, positively polarized. The yin side is about stepping back and gaining perspective. The yang side is about moving forward and taking action. The yin side often represents an inward emotion, usually about one's self or a feminine energy. The yang side can represent an emotion towards another or a masculine energy.

"Touch points" on the body send us messages about what's happening in our Physical, Emotional, Mental, and Spiritual bodies. It is a place where the physical and emotional come together – a trigger point. It can be useful to understand in two particular ways. First, when a point is touched and it is sore or tender, it may give us clues about "what's up" and assist us towards our healing. Second, touching that correlating point can assist in releasing and balancing the constricted energy (remember how interconnected the body, mind, emotions, and spirit are; helping one automatically helps the other). It can be beneficial to touch the point, feel the energy, and follow up with corresponding affirmations.

Using body mapping and touch points is very useful during a Breath session.

As a breather, understanding what's happening in your body is also helpful in helping to make positive changes in life.

Be sure that when using body mapping (or any other modality), you take it with a grain of salt and be open to different information and interpretation. For example, when I work out a lot, my chest gets very sore from weight lifting. If someone taps my touch points in my pectoral muscles, I scream with pain. Does it mean that I have compassion issues? However, when I have done breath sessions without workout muscle soreness and have been touched in the same places, I have felt incredible release and "aha" light bulb moments.

Shoulders:

Our shoulders literally bear heavy burdens when we feel anger towards someone or something, or when we hold too many people up. Resentment builds on the shoulders and so does stress and holding your breath.

Underneath the Ribs:

This in considered our fear belt. Four points on each side correspond to chakra issues. The two lower points would be lower chakra issues like survival, fear of life, fear of either receiving or expressing. It can also correlate to play, pleasure and power – fear of receiving or expressing those aspects of self through the inner child. The two upper points correspond to the upper chakra issues; love, higher will, and vision. Connected to the diaphragm, where there is often restriction, the fear belt is often sensetive to the touch, but also a powerful group of release points.

Hip Points:

The left points are related to the ability to be balanced and to move backward meaning reflective and inward. The right points are related to stepping forward in life and taking action. On the right side for example, someone who is particularly sensitive here may be having problems dealing with an issue about moving forward and taking action in their life.

Pubic Arch:

This central point located on the top and behind the pubic bone corresponds to judgments held around sexuality. The two points just left and right of the pubic arch are specific to male and female sexuality aspects of self.

Heart:

These points are located on either side of the sternum, moving up the rib cage between the ribs. They are located in the muscles between the ribs. Expressing and receiving love are the corresponding emotions.

Compassion Center:

These two points, located midway between the clavicle and the nipple on the chest, correspond to compassion about self and for others.

Body Mapping

Activate points with gentle to moderate pressure during exhale.
Use appropriate affirmations in conjunction with touch.

Front

Right Side
Expressive
Yang, Masculine,
Positively Polorized

Shoulder Points
Anger and resentment
toward others

Below Clavicals
Compassion for others

Points on Sternum
Expressing Love

Underneath Ribs
Fear Belt

Right Hip
Stepping Forward in
Life

Pubic Arch
Judgements about Sex
(Central bone on top
and behind bone on
either side)

Right Thigh
Male Self Image
(From inside knee
arching to hip)

Left Side
Receptive
Yin, Feminine,
Negatively Polorized

Shoulder Points
Anger and Resentment
Toward Self

Below Clavicals
Compassion for Self

Points on Sternum
Receiving Love

Underneath Ribs
Fear Belt

Left Hip
Stepping Back to
Gain Perspective

Left Thigh
Female Self Image
(From inside knee
arching to hip)

Calves
Receive Grounding
from earth and Anchor
Spirit to earth
(Points on back of calf
from knee to heel)

Circle Around Navel

A. Expression of Love and Power
B. Heart and Expression of Higher Will
C. Receptivity to Love and Power
D. Expression of Play, Pleasure, and Power
E. Survival Instinct
F. Receptivity to Play, Pleasure, and Power

Back Points
Beside Spine
Back points relate to
points on front with the
added emotion of guilt

Under Sit Bone
Negative thoughts
about self

138

Thighs:

These points lie inside the thigh, running in an arc from inside the knee to the hip. The points reflect self image. Left and right is associated with male and female aspects and moving forward or reflecting backward or inwardly.

Calves:

Located centrally from the knee to heel on the back side of the calf, these points are about our ability to ground and receive spirit (energy).

Back:

The points running along side the spine generally correlate to our chakras and the yin/yang energy thereof. Often associated with guilt, the back points are powerful release centers.

Sit Bone:

The four points of the sit bone reflect your opinion of yourself. Every time you think a negative thought about yourself it may show up as restricted energy here.

Buttocks and Neck:

The body is often times very literal. Who or what is a pain in your neck or ass is quite eye-opening, but usually fairly easy to identify. Don't forget to reflect upon yourself as being one of the largest contributors !!!

Using these touch points can be a powerful tool for release work and opening chi flow. A touch on the hip may allow someone to cry. A touch in the heart may bring someone a more compassionate thought. And a touch to the solar plexus can assist in letting go of fear or judgement.

Susan had pain when I touched her hip points and all around her lower abdomen. Later, I found out that she has endometriosis, horrendous painful menstrual cycles and she has been unable to get pregnant. However, she also has had a difficult time accepting her past and she is very afraid of her future. She has become, what she calls, a fatalist.

We have done a series of sessions and her cramps are much better. She uses the Breath for pain management and she is learning the touch points to help release the physical tension in her body. She's reading some wonderful books to help her understand the relationship between her outlook on life and her physical, emotional, mental, and spiritual well-being.

"I'm starting to understand that my physical ailments are connected with my holding on of the past. I worry about things all the time, but I realize that I can change this. Each Breath session that I do helps me feel a little safer and a little healthier. I feel like I'm beginning to heal. I know it's going to take time and work, but I think with all my new help, I can do it."

I came upon a map from many years ago from a massage therapist who practiced an old tradition of Hawaiian massage and energy work.

Body Mapping
Back

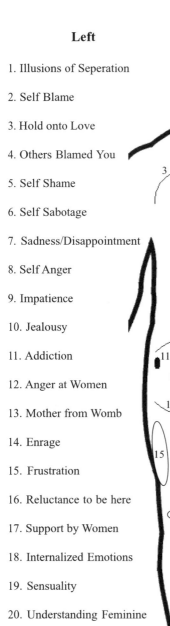

Left

1. Illusions of Seperation
2. Self Blame
3. Hold onto Love
4. Others Blamed You
5. Self Shame
6. Self Sabotage
7. Sadness/Disappointment
8. Self Anger
9. Impatience
10. Jealousy
11. Addiction
12. Anger at Women
13. Mother from Womb
14. Enrage
15. Frustration
16. Reluctance to be here
17. Support by Women
18. Internalized Emotions
19. Sensuality
20. Understanding Feminine

Right

21. Guilt
22. Gratitude
23. Control Issues
24. False Sense of Responsibility
25. Fear
26. Worry
27. Financial Concerns
28. Anger at Others
29. Revenge
30. Codependency
31. Anger at Men
32. Father Genetic
33. Letting Go
34. Outrage
35. Impatience
36. Procrastination
37. Support by Men
38. Internalized Negativity
39. Sexuality
40. Understanding Masculine

Affirmations for Breathing

Affirmations are positively reinforced statements that assist us in creating what we want and need in our lives. Napoleon Hill put it this way, "As a man thinketh, so he is." What we focus on in life is what we create. When we combine breath and affirmations, powerful transformation can occur.

Issue	Affirmation to Process Emotions
Chakra I and II	
Survival	I am safe
Emotions	It's safe for me to feel my emotions
Groundedness	It is safe to be in my body
Sexuality	It's safe in my belly
Seat of Subconscious	It's good to be me
Self-image	
Lower back pain, "Women issues," Mental issues, abundance issues, family issues	
Chakra III	
Separation of heart and will	My heart and will are one
Power judgements	It's easy to follow my heart (with my will)
Intellect	I rewrite my concept of power
Someone abused by power	God's will is my will
Strong willed parents	I am in charge of my life (so had to compensate and become "over-strong")
Chakra IV	
Giving and receiving love	I am loving, I am loved
It's not safe to feel in the heart	I don't have to DO anything to be loved
Strong willed parents (or others)	It is safe for me to open my heart
Chakra V	
Expression of Divine will	It is safe and easy to express myself
Expression	I feel the truth in my heart and all of who I am
	It is easy aligning Divine Will and my soul's vision

Compassion Centers
(located about two inches below the collar bone, centered on left and right side)

It is a place where we hold compassion for others, as well as inward compassion for our self.

Old sorrow	I forgive and release the past
Old grief	I let go and let God
Things that feel heavy on our chest	I surrender
	It's safe for me to love
	I am loved and cared for

Affirmations for Integrating the Breath

These affirmations can be used during a Life breath session. They assist in the transformational process and release work done during a session. They can also be used on a day to day basis to help transform your breath and your life.

To open the breath in our life	I am worthy.
	I accept my good.
	I am safe. I am secure.
To help resolve doubt	I am always cared for, always safe.
	I am blessed.
To help integrate heart and will	My heart and will are one.
	I am creativity.
To align Chakra II	I forgive and release the past.
	I am divine forgiveness.
	I forgive on whatever level I can now.
	It is safe to breathe into my belly.
To strengthen will	I am the only authority in my life.
	My will is free.
	I am strong.
	I am free now.
To balance the breath	I am perfect balance.
	I am in the flow.
	I am free to flow.
	I am balanced.
	My breath is balanced.
To relax the exhale	I relax my exhale to relax my life.
	It's safe for me to surrender.
	It is easy to let go now.
	It's safe to relax.

To Resolve Matters of the Heart	I breathe in love. I breathe in joy. I breath in peace. It is safe to open my heart. I am loved. I forgive and release the past.
To affirm truth in our life	I am as I was created. It is safe for me to stand in my truths. It's OK now. The truth can be safe now. I am the truth.
For accepting form	All I need is within me now.
For accepting form (Body / Self-worth)	It's safe to be in my body. My body is only my vessel. I accept my body as it is today. My past can not harm me now. The past is the past. It cannot harm me now.
To open the heart	My heart is filled with love and joy. I am loved and loving. My heart is opening now. It is safe in my heart. It is safe to breathe in my heart.
For accepting life more fully	It is safe for me to breathe. It is safe for me to live my life. I accept my life as it is today. It's OK. It's all OK.

In part, taken from International Breath Institute Training Material, Dr. Tom Goode, Dr. Judith Kravitz

Affirmations are very powerful. It is common for people to experience miraculous emotional release when I use words to help them let go. Mary held onto blame, guilt, fear, and anger around her relationship with her mother. During her session, I waited for the right time to verbalize, "I forgive and release the past. I surrender and I let go." She began repeating these phrases herself, over and over.

She shared, "All of a sudden I felt this wave come over my body. It was almost like a hot flash, but way more enjoyable. If I had to name it, I would call it a loving touch, but within the love was a sense of forgiveness. I never realized that it wasn't just my mother I had to forgive. I had to forgive ME! I blamed myself for allowing my mother to do all those things to me and then controlling me even now. I think I'm really on a new path. I think I get it. It doesn't matter what my mother does any more. What matters is how I respond to her and how I take care and love myself. Wow, who would have ever thought all this—just from breathing!"

Toning

Toning is making sound, which is a combination of vibration **and** energy. Toning can be used as a tool unto itself or it can be used in conjunction with Breathwork. Toning often helps move energy, especially during an intense wave of emotion or physical tension. Toning may occur naturally during a LifeBreath session or it may be encouraged to assist in the process of letting go.

Notes and tones can be held for long periods of time or they can be quick and sharp, sometimes loud, sometimes soft. It is beneficial to use the sound that connects you to release pent-up, overabundant or stagnant energy.

See exercise and chart on page 154 - 155.

It is sometimes beneficial for the breather to verbalize what he or she is going through or feeling. This is both beneficial for the breather as a tool for releasing, and for the facilitator, in helping to better understand what the breather is going through.

Note: **Too much** toning or talking during a session is discouraged and can actually distract from the session. When someone is talking, they are NOT breathing. And when someone is "over" toning or "faking," they may actually be holding on instead of releasing.

Laurie has only whispered for the last year. Her throat has become damaged from straining her vocal chords while teaching. She has been to many different kinds of doctors, but the medications have not helped yet. She is very frustrated and she can not work. Laurie has been taking Chi Kung with me for the last six months and is beginning to understand the power of the Breath. After our Chi Kung class, we usually practice LifeBreath for ten to fifteen minutes. During the classes we practice a technique called the "HA" breath. We inhale, and then yell HA as we exhale and "zap out" negative or pent-up energy. She can actually make sound. During the LifeBreath part, she gently tones and moves her attention to her throat. She affirms, "My throat center is open and balanced." After her Chi Kung class and LifeBreath sessions she can speak a few sentences without whispering.

Paul had some terrible memories of his childhood. He had difficulty showing his emotions and held onto his trauma mostly in his heart and throat. His inability to express was affecting all parts of his life — work, relationships, and his ability to find peace. During his LifeBreath sessions Paul began to slowly let go and create a new paradigm about his life. In the beginning, toning was out of the question. He was too embarrassed and fearful to make noise (after all, making noise used to get him in all kinds of trouble). During his third or fourth session,

Paul was really straining to keep his emotions down. His throat looked hard as a rock and he was literally swallowing his emotions down. Finally, he let out a little, tiny noise, and then another and another, getting a little louder each time. Towards the end of this release work, he began holding tones. This lasted a few minutes and then he began to cry. He finally mourned his past and began creating a new life. Paul's work, relationships, and love of himself are growing each day.

Reiki

Reiki (pronounced ray-key) is the laying-on of hands for healing. It was allegedly originated as a Tibetan Buddhist practice that was rediscovered in the late 1800's by Dr. Makao Usui. "Rei" means Universal Spirit and "Ki" means life force energy. It is very simple and yet powerful. While creating a harmonious balance within the PEMS systems, it allows true healing from within to occur.

We can use Reiki during a breath session to enhance the work that is being done through breath. We call our Reiki, "Intuitive Reiki." We *lay hands* where it feels right. We also *lay hands* where we want to work with loving energy. Breathing analysis and watching the breath can help show us the areas to place our hands. For instance, if someone is not breathing in their belly, by placing my hand there, I encourage energy and breath to support that area. It helps remind the breather to breathe there and it also places attention and loving energy into that spot. It is very common for people to believe that my hand is still there minutes, even an hour after I have moved. This *is* the energy (which is universal chi). It can feel very loving and supportive. As a Reiki practitioner, I am only a conduit of the universe's energy.

Reiki…
Releases stress and pain	Relaxes muscle spasms
Releases emotional blockages	Accelerates natural healing
Stimulates the immune system	Balances subtle body energies

Bill is a wonderful, jovial Santa Claus kind of guy. When people meet him, they instantly feel his energy. Inside, he has some turmoil. He is a recovering alcoholic who has shifted his life toward helping people and teaching. He is on a positive path and continues his upward spiral.

During one of his sessions, I placed my hands on his heart and felt such a sense of unconditional love and openness. At that moment, I saw this incredible smile come upon his face and his hands went to my hands. We embraced the moment. After his session, he shared the experience of feeling love. He said his heart was opened. He shared that even after I left the room, my hands were still there. He explained that, ever since, his heart has remained more open and his life feels more unconditional and loving.

Tapping

I sometimes use a technique called "tapping." I gently tap on and around an energy center or touch point to help wake it up, open it, or draw attention to it.

Tapping is quite comforting and feels good. Tapping can also be used to help congestion around the lungs, both on the back and front of the rib cage. I often use stroking on the throat instead of tapping because it is more comforting and gentle.

When Sally was about halfway into her breath session, I could see and hear that her upper chest and throat were closed. I began gently tapping the center of her chest and then stroking her throat. I could tell that it was making her feel more relaxed and safe. She began to quietly tone and then eventually opened her toning a little louder. I sensed a real release occurring. Afterwards, toward the end of the session, Sally looked extremely relaxed and her breathing was easy, flowing and naturally circular. She rested a long while in this state. When Sally returned from this state of bliss, she shared her experience.

"When I first started to breathe I kinda wondered when anything would start to kick in and then all of a sudden...BAM... I was vibrating, tingling, and energized. About halfway through, I felt like the breath was stopping just below my chest. It felt like it was getting into my belly and up into the lower part of the chest and then it actually hurt to bring it up further. My heart hurt. Then my throat started to restrict and tighten. I felt sad and a little scared. When Beth began to tap on my chest and stroke my throat, I was able to let go. I cried out that ball in my throat and the pressure in my chest. When I started to make the sound that Beth encouraged, it felt sooo good to let it all go. After I sounded out, I got lost in this beautiful peaceful place. I don't know where I went. I was sooo relaxed. It was wonderful. I've never felt so peaceful in my whole life."

Prayer and Conscious Intention

Many of us understand the power of prayer. It is the power of intention multiplied by the power of God (nature, spirit, universal chi, or whatever *you* call it). When I facilitate, I quietly pray. Quite often breathers instinctively pray as well.

Ronnie didn't consider himself a religious man, but after his experience during a LifeBreath session, he definitely considers himself connected and spiritual. Watching his session, I could see a sense of peace come over his body. He was skeptical when he first started doing his session, but he was willing to put the effort into breathing.

Here's what Ronnie said afterwards:

"I think I saw the eyes of God. I can't believe it. I actually saw it. I'll be! I saw it! I feel wonderful! I think my life is taking an incredible turn. I'll never forget this. Thank you, God."

Section III

Life Exercises

Exercises that Change the Way We Live

*Just as physical exercise changes our body,
mental/emotional/spiritual activities transform us too.*

Here is a collection of my favorite life altering exercises.

Conscious Breathing Techniques

Throughout this book we have talked about conscious breathing. We established that natural healthy breathing is through the nose, relaxed, full, subtle, and circular. The LifeBreath Technique is dynamic, breathing usually through the mouth, circular, and it's used as a powerful transformational tool.

There are many other breathing modalities used to invoke different responses and create subtly altered states of mind.

Cleansing Breath

Used for cleansing and calming our thoughts when we are overly excited, nervous, stressed out, or just want to focus better. I often start my Chi Kung, aerobic, or meditation sessions with a few cleansing breaths. It's a great way to wake up in the morning or go to sleep at night. I would recommend it for overcoming fear and for anger management as well.

- In through the nose. Take a nice long extended inhale.
- Out through the mouth, nice and long and steady. (No holds)
- 3 – 21 repetitions

Oxygenating Health Breath

Used a few times a day to increase oxygen flow to the brain and blood stream. It can be used to lead into meditation.

- In through the nose for a count of 4
- Hold for a count of 16 (or as long as you are comfortable, do not force)
- Out through the nose for a count of 8 (again, do not force, be comfortable)
- 3-21 repetitions

Relaxation Breath

RELAX! This breath can be used to prepare for meditation, rest or sleep.

- Exhale through the mouth making a *whoosh* sound
- Gently close your mouth.
- Count 4 on the inhale through the nose
- Hold for 7 counts
- Exhale, *whoosh*, through the mouth again
- Repeat five or more times

Yin Yang Breath
"Alternating nostril breath"

Used for calming, balancing, and clearing the head.

Himalyan Yogis maintained that Yin/Yang Breathing, or alternate nostril breathing, is essential for ascending to higher mental and spiritual planes. They believed right nostril breathing balanced active or agressive instincts and left nostril breathing induced more passive behavior. Present research about the right and left brain support their theories.

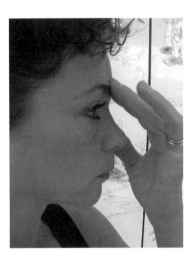

Variation I:
Place one hand in front of your face with the pointer and middle finger on the third eye (between the brow). Place your thumb over one nostril and the ring finger by the other.

- Hold one nostril
- Exhale 4 counts
- Hold 4 counts
- Inhale 4 counts
- Hold 4 counts
- Switch to opposite nostril
- Repeat these cycles for one to ten minutes

Variation II:
- Use the same hand position as Variation I, but just breathe in and out of one nostril 10 - 21 times.
- Switch and breathe in and out of the other nostril 10 - 21 times (No holding).

Kundalini Breathing with Movement

Used to energize, exercise, get moving and motivated. Also used to move the Kundalini energy up through the spine and chakras.

Kundalini

For LifeBreath purposes, we use Kundalini breathing to energize a Breath session and/or to raise our vital energy level in general. Kundalini is the energy that often lays dormant at the base of the spine. As we grow towards a more enlightened state of being, the energy climbs up the spine and chakra ladder.

This breath is executed in and out of the mouth and diaphragmatically, so that the belly raises on the inhale and falls on the exhale. It is often done while standing and raising the arms overhead on the inhale and lowering the arms on the exhale. It's fun to do to music and can be quite aerobic and invigorating. Used at the beginning of a LifeBreath session, it creates a state of high energy and enthusiasm. It assists in starting the session in a more vital, energized, and open manner.

- In and out through the mouth
- Raise hands over head on the inhale
- Hands come down on the exhale
- Breathe fully (belly to heart)

Great to music and movement.
Wonderful in group settings

Ha Breath

Used to release stress while toning.
Lots of fun, kids love it, immediate stress reducer.

- Raise arms and shoulders and breathe in through the nose
- Quickly and loudly say "HA" on the exhale (quickly) and flick hands downward
- Repeat three to seven times.

Boogie Breath

Used to get you "rocking and rolling" and excited. Great for indoor recess. Kids love it!

This breath is done in through the nose and out through the mouth.

- Begin to rock hands and body up and out, rolling onto the balls and heels of the feet.
- Arms go up on breath in; roll onto your toes.
- Arms go down on breath out; roll onto your heels.

Rocking on the heels and balls stimulates all the nerve endings and accupressure points on the bottom of the feet. This is an all around beneficial exercise for anyone to do.

Variation:

- Jumping on the upward movement can be added for extra excitement and energy.

Belly Only Breath

Used to access feelings and energy around the first, second, and third chakra.

Done through the mouth, the same as Lifebreath; however, breathe into the belly only. The breath is fluid, robust, with a focused inhale and a relaxed exhale. Keep the heart silent and relaxed. This is a very effective breath for moving energy into the lower chakra.

Heart Only Breath

Done exactly as described above except heart only, no belly breath. This is effective for moving energy into the heart and resolving matters around the fourth chakra.

Toning Exercises

Toning is an ancient art of making sound that helps release and transform energy. Toning exercises are automatically associated with our breathing patterns because we must breathe in order to tone. Making sound is vibrational and the resonation can help shift our energy.

Hu:
This is an ancient sound for power, pronounced "Hugh." This can be chanted silently or stated aloud during the exhale. If stated aloud, only execute a maximum of fifteen repetitions. *It really is very powerful.*
Try inhaling through the nose and exhaling aloud or silently. Then try inhaling and exhaling through the nose while silently saying, "HU."

Hoo:
Used like Hu, pronounced "Who"

Ani-hu (anee-who):
Done for compassion, empathy, and unity. Again, this can be done silently or as a chant. It makes a very powerful group chant.

Ra (rah):
If you want lots of energy, try this one. Inhale, then try saying "rrraaaaahhhh" on your exhale throughout the entire exhale. Then... *Watch Out !!!!*

So-hawng (soe-hung):
This keeps your mind busy if you tend to be someone who has a hard time focusing during meditation.

Tho (though):
This is a tone for healing. It is pronounced "thooooooo," with the emphasis on the "o" throughout the exhale. Try sending the energy to a special life issue or a place in your body that needs healing.

HangSah (hang-saahhh):
Inwardly say "Hang" on the inhale and "saaaaaahhhhh" on the exhale. The "sah" can be silent or aloud. This keeps the mind active and helps us connect to our highest concept of goodness. It's a powerful mantra leading into and/or during meditation.

Here is a chart of the basic note, sound, color, energy, and location of each chakra.

Chakra	Note/Sound	Color	Energy	Location
1	Hi C / Uhhhh	Red	Life Force	Base of spine
2	C / Oooo	Orange	Sex	Abdomen
3	F / Ho	Yellow	Power	Solar Plexus
4	Hi E / Ahhh	Green	Balance	Heart
5	G / A	Blue	Will	Throat
6	A/ Eeee	Indigo	Vision	Brow
7	D / Mmmm	Violet	Spirit	Crown

LifeBreath Style Tai Chi / Chi Kung

The force we call Chi (Qi) is also used to describe air, breath, and internal energy. It is the fundamental life energy of the universe. Gong (kung) represents work or achievement.

**Chi Kung is the practice of working with
Breath and Universal Life Energy.**

Chi Kung practices are used to gain control over the forces of energy in our bodies. The exercises can be used as a daily routine to increase overall health and well being, mental control, emotional clarity, and spiritual connection. Much like the LifeBreath Technique, Chi Kung is powerful and profound *"medicine."* Through these exercises, we learn to discover, gather, circulate, purify, direct, conserve, store, transform, dissolve, and transmit chi.

Chi cultivation can be used to resolve challenges or to enhance any living function. Used consistently, Chi Kung practitioners experience improved health and greater access to power and energy.

**By adjusting and regulating our body's posture and movement,
breathing patterns, and consciousness (or thought), we make
accessible to us the heavenly elixir of chi.**

—Photo by Robin Leavitt

We are born with inherited amounts of chi, but we acquire it from air, water, food, and even sunlight, in which chi is all present. It travels along channels called meridians. There are twelve main meridians, corresponding to the twelve principal organs defined by traditional Chinese systems: the lung, large intestines, stomach, spleen, heart, small intestine, urinary bladder, kidney, liver, gallbladder, pericardium, and the "triple warmer." Each of our organs has chi associated with it, along with corresponding emotional and mental energy. Chi Kung exercise influences the flow of chi and the organ and meridian health.

The concept of Yin/Yang also plays an integral role in understanding the balance of energy in our bodies. The universe is divided into two separate, but complementary, interacting energies with vast implications. Chi Kung helps balance these energies and assists in making us whole.

**Here are a few of my favorite simple, but profound
Tai Chi /Chi Kung exercises:**
(For visual instructions, a LifeBreath Chi Kung video is available):

Standing Meditation and Rooting

This practice allows you to become rooted and yet connected to the heavens at the same time. Through standing meditation, you can tap into the energy of the earth, as well as the energy from the universe.

Execution:
- Find a quiet, peaceful place to stand.
- Place your left hand and then your right hand over your lower belly with your thumbs by your navel.
- Gently close your eyes.
- Become mindful of your breathing.
- Imagine that there is a hollow tube running from your nostrils down into your belly where your hands are. At the end of the hollow tube, imagine a balloon. Each time you inhale, allow the balloon to inflate, bringing your belly outward along with it. And, on the exhale, let the belly fall. Allow the breath to become open, circular, easy and full. Now bring the breath up from the belly into your heart like a wave. Begin low and raise the breath up. Continue to bring the breath in and out in a circular manner with no pauses between the inhale and the exhale.
- Relax the body by relaxing the toes, feet, ankles, and calves.
- Keep the knees gently bent and breathe through your nose.

- Relax the thighs, hips, lower back, and lower belly.
- Spend some extra time relaxing the diaphragm, a place where we often hold tension.
- Relax the middle back, chest, and upper back.
- Continue to breathe and relax the shoulders, arms, and hands.
- Relax the neck, forehead, cheeks, and even the jaw.
- So, from the tips of your toes to the top of your head, just relax.
- *It's a very peaceful feeling to be so deeply relaxed.*
- Focus your attention on the bottom of your feet.
- Feel the bottom of your feet and imagine ...
- There are roots growing from the bottom of your feet deep into the earth.
- These roots are growing longer and stronger and healthier with each breath in and out.
- Imagine that these roots are drawing you downward towards the center of the earth as they grow.
- The bottom half of your body may feel slightly heavy, grounded, rooted to the earth.
- You might like to imagine that from these roots you are receiving vital nutrients from the earth that replenish and rejuvenate you. You draw in life energy.
- Continue to breathe – relax and remain grounded.
- Focus your attention on your spine, neck, and head.
- Imagine them elongating towards the sky as though someone is gently lifting you upwards, making your spine erect and yet relaxed. Feel the spine drawing upward.
- You might like to imagine that there is energy pouring over you and through you from the heavens above, showering you with white light and vital chi.
- Remain grounded and yet light and connected.
- Continue to relax and breathe.
- Remain in standing meditation for 5 minutes to an hour.

To come out of the session
- Ever so slowly and gently, open your eyes and place your hands gently in front of your thighs.
- Let your hands hang for a moment and feel them being pulled downward, as they lay limp.
- You may want to take a few deep cleansing breaths.

Discovering Chi

In order to work with your energy, you must discover it before you can cultivate it. This exercise helps you capture and FEEL the force.

Execution:
- Execute Standing Meditation and Rooting.
- Place your hands in a gentle ball-like circle in front of you; keep your hands completely relaxed. Meditate on the chi flowing through your body and into your circle. This exercise can be executed for two to thirty minutes. It is beneficial to discover your chi, consciously bringing energy into your body, so that you can learn to balance and distribute the energy for health and well-being.
- You can put your attention to different energy centers while discovering your chi. You can focus on drawing energy from the roots of your feet, from the heavenly energy through the top of your head, or you can focus on the energy vibration between your hands and arms.
- You may experience energy pulsating through your hands, arms, and even throughout your entire body. It can feel like heat, tingling, pulsating, and a sense of buzzing and vibrating.
- You may vary this by standing in a horse riding stance. This is very grounding and it also creates very strong legs.

Standing Meditation and Circulating Chi Through the Microcosmic Orbit

Two major meridians, the front and back channels, make up the microcosmic orbit. There are fourteen major points that relate to all major functions of the body in this circle. By focusing on the orbit and your breath, you help restore balance and harmony back into the body.

Microcosmic Orbit

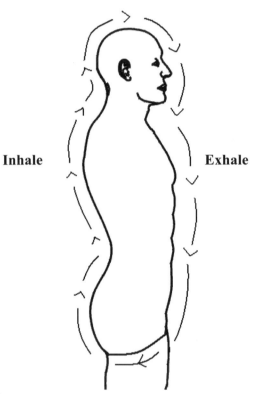

Inhale · Exhale

Execution:
- Execute Standing Meditation and Rooting.
- Focus your breath and your energy through the microcosmic orbit.
- Follow the line of energy from your tan tien (second chakra), up through the torso and spine, over your head, then down the middle line of the front of your torso, and back to the tan tien. Inhale as you visualize the upward movement of the orbit and exhale as your focus travels down your torso.

This exercise is beneficial to learn how to circulate energy through your body, chakras, and associated organs.

Variation: Breathe in through the nose and out through the mouth.

Zap – Discovering Chi

The "Zap" exercise is another way to discover chi.

Execution:
Extend your arms and hands in front of your body and make a tight fist. Then quickly release the fist and zap your fingers out. Do this about thirty times, fast, with your palms down. Then flip your palms up and fist and zap another thirty quick times. Now, form a ball with your hands and arms bent in front of you like you're holding a basketball ready to throw. Totally relax your hands and arms. Close your eyes and FEEL the energy in your hands and arms. Move the ball slightly smaller and larger and FEEL the magnetic pull. You may feel tingling, heat, or sense an energy between your hands. This is living "CHI."

Transmitting Chi

Used as a powerful self-help tool, transmitting chi is commonly practiced for health maintenance and healing. It is essentially Reiki, the laying on of hands or healing touch. Chi can be transmitted through touch and/or conscious thought. The more "clear" your energy (less restriction, more flow, not an over abundance), the more power you have to transmit chi.

Execution:
- Execute Standing Meditation and Rooting and Discover Chi or Zap.
- Place your hands on any part of your body you'd like to transmit/send energy to. Visualize the energy being sent. Feel the energy.
- This can be done seated, standing, or lying.

Example: If you have an injured shoulder, place your hand(s) on your shoulder. If you would like to open your heart chakra, place your hands on your heart.

"Transmitting chi" and "directing chi" can be done by first zapping and/or rubbing the hands together, then directing the loving energy to someone else or to yourself. You can also send a general "Intention" to someone. For example, you can send love, light, healing energy, or peace out to another person or out into the world in general.

Awakening Chi

By breathing deeply and visualizing the energy flowing through the body, you can begin to awaken the sleeping chi within you. This is a powerful exercise to draw energy from your roots, balance your breathing, coordinate the body/mind/spirit and learn "flow."

Execution:
- Begin with the standing meditation
- Rest your hands by your thighs and stand with your feet about shoulder width apart. Draw your hands upward in front of you, leading by the wrists, hands limp, while inhaling. Draw the hands downward, leading through the elbows while exhaling. Make the movement and the breath circular. Allow the body to rise and fall slightly with the movement by straightening and bending at the knee, keeping the back straight. From the tips of your toes to the top of your head and through your fingertips, you are circulating breath and chi and you are undulating with movement. Relax all parts of the body and only recruit the muscles that are needed to move. Allow your PEMS bodies to awaken to the energy.
- Finish with a few minutes of standing meditation.

Gathering Earth Energy

This exercise creates a powerful energy transfusion from the earth to you. You draw on the chi from mother nature and consciously bring it into your body.

Execution:
- Ground yourself with your feet about two shoulder widths apart, with your knees slightly bent. Keep your back straight and on a parallel plane with your legs. As you inhale through your nose, draw in the energy first from the earth and your roots, then through your feet and into your body. Bend at the knees and draw your hands into a scooping motion, as though you were picking up a ball and raising it chest high. Bring your hands to the center of your chest, then imagine exhaling out through your heart as you execute a breast stroke-like movement with your hands. You may exhale through the nose or the mouth. As you bend and inhale, keep your back straight and perpendicular to the floor. Straighten your legs slightly on the inhale and bend on the exhale. Imagine drawing the energy up through the body, then dispursing it through your heart to help open up your heart energy. You might like to imagine filling your body up with earth's energy or, perhaps, white healing light.
- Repeat this between three and twenty-one times.
- Then, continue this same movement, but bring it up through the heart and overhead like a giant star burst, drawing your hands overhead and then to your sides. Imagine drawing the energy from your roots all the way up through the top of your head. Continue to gather energy from the earth.
- Repeat this between three and twenty-one times also.
- Finish with a few minutes of standing meditation.

Gathering Universal Energy
Gather energy from the heavens.

Execution:
- Reverse the direction of Gather Earth Energy to draw the chi from around you and above you. Palms are up on the inhale, drawing the energy up and in as you raise your hands overhead. As you exhale, face the palms downward and gently draw the arms down in front of your body. Image that the hands draw the energy into your body. Repeat this 3 to 21 times.
- As you come to closure with this exercise, slow it down, exhale very slowly and distribute the gathered chi into the entire body by visualizing the chi throughout the body.
- Finish with a few minutes of standing meditation.

Trunk Rolls

There are many benefits to this simple exercise:
- Stimulating foot reflexology points
- Strengthening of the muscles
- Improving oxygenation and blood flow
- Creating stronger bones and a healthier heart
- Lubricating and stimulating the spine
- Relaxing and stretching the neck and shoulder muscles
- Stimulating and massaging the organs

This is a wonderful way to start and end your day. Performing a few times throughout the day helps keep you relaxed and loose. I recommend this for anyone who sits at a desk or stands for long periods of time. Every half hour to hour, stand up and do a few minutes of trunk rolls. You may be surprised. Over time, you may not suffer the detrimental effects that are usually inevitable from standing or sitting for prolonged periods.

I have had great success working with athletes using the trunk roll as a warm up for golf, tennis, martial arts, and any kind of physical performance.

Execution:
- Stand with your legs about shoulder width apart and begin to swing your arms side to side by allowing your hips to engine and propel the movement. Trunk rolls can be done slowly to relax you or they can be done quickly to help energize you. It can be performed with the feet grounded to the earth or by twisting and allowing the feet to turn in the direction that your body turns.
- Allow your arms to just flop side to side – no tension, no control.

Cleansing the Lungs

Stagnant air left in the lungs due to shallow breathing can be cleansed through deep breathing. Most people only use a small percentage of their lung capacity each day, so, by drawing deep down, we can improve our lung capcity and clean out the old air.

Execution:
- Draw the inhale through the nose as you gather energy. Bring your hands in front of you in a scooping manner from below your navel upwards to your heart, with your palms up. Then exhale out through the mouth and extend your arms out to the side, palms pushing outward. The inhale is drawn fairly quickly and the exhale is pushed out with some force, contracting the abdominal muscles and pushing the hips slightly forward until the lungs are **completely** emptied. Allow your body to become concave as you allow all the air to be expelled.
- This exercise should only be done a few times and only once or twice a day. It helps detoxify the body and cleanses stagnant carbon dioxide out of the lower lungs.

Cleansing Your Aura

Execute Cleansing the Lungs, but in a very gentle, slow, and soft way. Then continue the circular movements and draw your arms overhead, in front and downward. Imagine breathing in radiant, healthy energy distributing throughout your body, then exhale and push away (side, front, overhead, and below) any negativity or unbalanced or restricted energy.

Meditation

Modern medicine and technology are catching up to what people from all over the world and all walks of life have been saying for thousands of years. *Meditation is really good for us.* Not only will you find meditation being practiced for wellness and health in general, physicians are now recommending it to prevent, slow, and control the pain of many chronic diseases. It is also being highly endorsed to restore balance to psychiatric disturbances like depression, ADD, manic behavior, and stress related disorders. Many of us relate meditation to its mystical and spiritual aspects, but meditation is being proven to alter not only the thinking mind, but amazingly, to reshape the physical brain.

There are many styles of meditation, but the key is to pick one and DO IT. When we are **quiet**, life has a chance to speak to us in a still, silent voice *(or not so silent sometimes)*. Insight and awareness come through to guide us in every part of life. We can alter and transform our mind, body and spirit through meditation. We may experience revelations, light bulb moments, *aha's*, or simply, peace of mind.

Most of us perform a kind of meditation when we are engrossed in one deliberate thought or action. Time has a way of slipping away and we are completely focused and concentrated. However, taking time to "just be" or focus on higher intentions is considered *conscious meditating*.

Getting Started

A great way to begin conscious meditation is by simply closing your eyes and becoming aware of your breath. You don't necessarily need to change your breathing, just become aware of it and watch it. In and out, in and out, rising and falling.

Then imagine that there is a hollow tube from your nose going deep into your belly about two inches below your navel. At the end of the hollow tube imagine a balloon. As you inhale into the balloon, your belly will rise outward and expand. As you gently exhale, the balloon and your belly will fall. Just focus on your breathing and give your body and mind the command to relax. You may want to go through each body part, starting at your toes, and consciously relax each part. Move all the way up to your head and out through your hands.

Once you've relaxed, allow your mind to empty into "nothingness." Allow any thoughts to just come and go. Do not force them away. Just let them go. Listen for insights or guidance.

Postures for Meditation

(You may also lie down comfortably.)

Alpha Induction:
(Please note that I have created an audio tape/ CD for this style of meditation)

In order to set the stage for meditation, it is essential to allow your mind and body to become relaxed. This state of mind, called an alpha state, is a time when you are very open. An example of the alpha state is the feeling you get just before you fall asleep and when you first awaken.

You can read through this exercise and then begin to put yourself into an alpha state. It takes some practice, but the benefits are substancial.

Sit comfortably, with spine upright and your hands resting lightly on your thighs. The hands can be placed palm up or down. If need be, you may also lie down comfortably.

While breathing in and out through your nose, begin to focus inwardly and give your body the command to relax. Imagine that there is a hollow tube running from your nose deep into your belly to a few inches below your navel. At the end of the hollow tube, imagine that there is a balloon. On each inhale allow the belly and the balloon to expand. And on each exhale allow the belly and the balloon to fall. Allow the breath to flow upward to your heart. Relax the exhale and let the breath fall from the belly and heart naturally.

To enter a deep and healthy level of mind, close your eyes and take a few deep breaths into your belly and heart. While exhaling, mentally repeat the word RELAX several times, then DEEPER several times, then HEALTHIER several times. Allow yourself to enter a deeper and healthier level of mind. Deeper and healthier than before. Continue to breathe and relax.

To assist you to reach a deeper and healthier level of mind, count backwards from twenty to ten. With each descending number, feel yourself become more relaxed, healthier and deeper in your state of mind. Continue to breathe ... Going backward now 20, 19, 18 ... more and more relaxed ... 17, 16, 15 ... healthier and healthier ... 14, 13, 12 ... deeper and deeper ... 11 ... 10. You are now at a deeper and healthier level of mind, deeper and healthier than before. Relax ...

**To enter a deeper and healthier level of mind,
all you have to do is imagine ...**

your **hands and arms** *to be completely relaxed and you will automatically enter a deeper and healthier level of mind. Relax your hands and arms and place these parts of the body into a state of deep relaxation that will become deeper as you go deeper.*

Relax your arms completely ... deeper and deeper, healthier and healtheir, more and more relaxed.

Relax your **feet, calves and legs** *... deeper and deeper, healthier and healtheir, more and more relaxed.*

Relax your **hips, lower back and lower belly** *... deeper and deeper, healthier and healtheir, more and more relaxed.*

Relax your **diaphragm and middle back** *... deeper and deeper, healthier and healtheir, more and more relaxed.*

*Relax your **chest, upper back and shoulders** ... deeper and deeper, healthier and healthier, more and more relaxed.*

*Relax your **neck** completely.*

*Relax your **jaw and mouth, forehead, and eyelids** and place these parts of the body into a state of deep relaxation that will become deeper as you go deeper.*

*Take a few deep breaths and relax **your entire spine.** Imagine relaxing your **organs and cells** and let them resume their natural, rhythmic functioning.*

So, from the tips of your toes to the top of your head you are completely relaxed. Feel a sense of deep relaxation descend upon the entire body. Relax, it is a very peaceful feeling to be so deeply relaxed.

(This is where you would implement various creative visualizations and deeper meditation)

To come out of an alpha state:

It is time to come back from (that peaceful place)

Counting from one to five, with each ascending number you will feel more awake, energized, and recharged...

Coming up slowly now.

One ... feel the life force coming back to your hands and arms.

Feel the life force coming back to your feet and toes.

Two ... feel the life force coming back into your neck and shoulders, legs and hips. Slowly coming back now.

Three ... feel the life force coming back into your chest and back ... into your belly.

Four ... feel the life force coming back into your jaw and mouth, forehead and eyelids ... slowly coming back ... slowly opening your eyes.

Five ... fully back, feeling calm and relaxed yet energized.

A Few Favorite Meditations and Creative Visualization Exercises

Triune Breath and Meditation

This breathing technique connects your higher energy centers and bypasses the astral realms to allow you to consciously participate with the higher dimensions of your being. It is a very powerful, guided breathing technique that assists you in connecting with the more spiritual parts of your life. It was introduced to me through the Cosmic Breath Institute in 1996 by Dr. Tom Goode and Dr. Judith Kravitz.

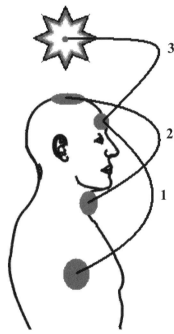

Triune Breath

Execution:
- Create an alpha state through the Alpha Induction Exercise or any other modality. Give your body the command to completely relax, take a few deep breaths through your nose and close your eyes.
  (You may want to use your hand the first few times you do this and place it in the area where you are holding your consciousness as indicated below).
- In your mind's eye, imagine inhaling through your **heart** chakra and exhaling through your **third eye** (located between the brows).

- Now, imagine inhaling through your **throat** chakra and exhaling through the **crown** chakra *(located about six inches above your head)*.
- Lastly, imagine inhaling through your **third eye** and exhaling through the **soul star** chakra (located twelve to eighteen inches above your head). Hold the image of the great central sun with the brightness equivalent to sixteen suns.
- Repeat this exercise seven times.
- Then hold onto the energy as long as you need to in order to feel complete.

Third Eye Breath and Meditation

Breathing through your third eye is an exercise that evokes higher consciousness and intuition.

Execution:
- Place yourself into an alpha state. Sit up tall, feet resting on the ground, hands gently on your thighs.

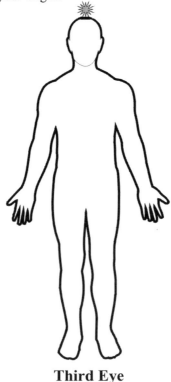

Third Eye

- Take a deep breath and hold it gently, then exhale. Another, hold it, let go, and shift focus.
- Begin to use your mind's eye to breath in and out through your third eye while, breathing through your nose.

- Visualize light entering the third eye while focusing on and repeating the word "ONE."
- Continue until you feel complete. Colors, lights, shapes, guides, energy, intuition, and insights are common.

Put yourself into a relaxed state of mind, an alpha state, then ...

Affirmation Meditation

Focus on a particular positive affirmation or view a situation from your mind's eye. Bring it up into your meditation and allow intuition guide you.

A Little Piece of Heaven

Focus on a place where you feel very safe and beautiful, perhaps a mountain top, a beach, or surrounded by loving souls. Then, experience what it feels like to be in that loving place and go there any time you want that feeling.

Calling Forward Spiritual Guidance

Consciously ask for help in your meditation. Call upon your guides, angels, or Higher Power.

Angel Massage

Imagine being surrounded by angels and allow them to go through your different body parts and give their divine touch.

If this sounds a little too far out there, just try it, it's actually very pleasant.

Body Scanning

Scan your body. Begin by becoming aware of your breath. Observe your breath and FEEL where it goes and how that feels. Can you feel which parts of your body move? Can you feel where the breath goes? Is there anywhere the breath feels tighter than in other places? Become aware of that. Feel the tightness and ask, "What is that about? Do I feel any emotion connected to that area?" Then send it loving energy.

Now, just become aware of your entire body. Is there anywhere you feel tight? Is there anywhere you feel unusual? Is there any emotion connected to that area?

This is a great way to start your day. Lie in bed, breathe a few minutes and do a body scan and ask, "What's up?"

Body scanning can be done anywhere. Remember, being AWARE of a problem is the first step to a solution. Your body can never lie to you. When you become "One" with it, it can become a true friend. When we struggle against it or against life itself, it can feel like a foe.

CHAKRA Alignment / Attunement
(Please note that I have created an audio tape / CD for this exercise)

When we meditate on the chakras, we can assist in opening their energy through our conscious intention and by breathing into them. We can dedicate an entire meditation session on one chakra, a group of chakra or all the chakras.

Using the open mouth LifeBreath Technique while focusing on each chakra is a powerful variation. For a more subtle meditation, you may breathe through your nose.

Here is an example of the wording I use for the first chakra. You can *play with* the wording for the other chakras to suit your individual needs. You can also physically place your hand(s) where the chakra is located:

Breathe into the first chakra, located at the base of the spine. Imagine a glowing red ball there filled with energy. Imagine that the energy is getting healthier, more vibrant, and alive.

It is in this center that we hold our life force. It is here where we hold our tribal and family beliefs. Safety, security, and our grounding are held here. The qualities of justice, honor, and loyalty also eminate from this space. Our basic human instincts reside here too.

Let's allow any emotions or issues around this area to come forward and ask for healing and forgiveness.

I affirm that...

My 1st chakra is open and balanced.
I am cared for and I am loved.
I feel at home with myself.
I feel firmly planted.
I am safe in my physical body.

This can be done with each chakra. Learn what each chakra represents and you can make up your own alignment exercises.

Also, start becoming aware of how your chakra centers feel. Know how you respond to life within your body. You will begin to automatically check in with your body and tap into intuition through this awareness. For example, when my children are upset, I feel it in my third chakra. I can physically feel their pain. I check in with the feeling and work on using my intuition and I try to learn the lesson I am being taught.

Here's a list of each chakra, its location, color, basic energy, sacred truth, and some sample affirmations:

Remeber to BREATHE into the center.

Chakra I

Location: Base of the spine
Color: Red
Sacred Truth: *"All is one"*

Energy:

Life Force	Physical	Instinctual
Tibal/Family	Security	Safety
Survival	Groundedness	Balance
Loyalty	Justice	Honor

Affirmations for the first chakra
- My 1st chakra is open and balanced.
- I am cared for. I am loved.
- I feel at home with myself.
- I feel firmly planted.
- I am safe in my physical body.

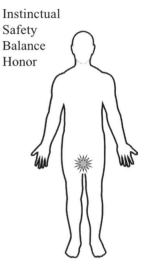

Chakra II

Location: About two inches below the naval / Sacral
Color: Orange
Sacred Truth: *"Honor one another"*

Energy:

Control	Boundaries	Survival Instincts
Relationships	Financial Energy	Work Ethics
Personal Power	Creativity	Risk Taking
Worthiness	Self Image	Creative Energy
Work	Relationships	
Sexuality	Physical Desire	

Affirmations for the second chakra
- I am always safe.
- I honor myself and others.
- My 2nd chakra is open and balanced.
- It is safe for me to feel pleasure.
- I feel at home in my body.
- I trust myself and my instincts.

Chakra III

Location: Solar Plexus
Color: Yellow
Sacred Truth: *"Honor oneself"*

Energy:
Personal Power	Self-Esteem	Self-Responsibility
Self-Respect	Self-Discipline	Ambition
Courage	Generosity	Ethics
Fear	Personal Identity	Power
Intellectual/Mental Energy		

Affirmations for the third chakra
- I am perfect and whole just as I am
- I like myself.
- I respect myself.
- I am following my passion.
- I am not to judge. I am open.
- My 3rd chakra is open and balanced.
- I create a positive environment for myself every day.
- I am impeccably honest with myself and others.

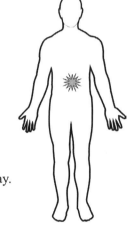

Chakra IV

Location: Heart
Color: Green
Sacred Truth: *"Love is divine power"*

Energy:
Love	Forgiveness	Compassion
Inspiration	Trust	Healing
Dedication	Hope	Harmony
Issues of the Soul	Giving and Receiving Love	

Affirmations for the fourth chakra
- The past does NOT equal the future.
- I am loved.
- I am loving.
- I am safe.
- I choose love over fear.
- My Heart is open and balanced.
- I am abundantly loved.
- I trust.
- I freely forgive myself.
- I forgive.

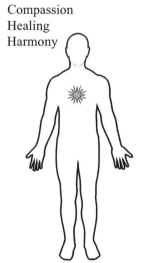

Chakra V

Location: Throat
Color: Blue
Sacred Truth: *"I surrender Divine Will to my personal will"*

Energy:

Higher Will	Faith	Personal
Knowledge	Personal Authority	Surrender
Self-Expression	Choice and Consequences (karma)	
Creative Expression	Communication	

Affirmations for the fifth chakra
- My 5th chakra is open and balanced.
- I communicate clearly and easily.
- I trust my creative intuition.
- I follow the path of my highest good.
- I receive intuition.
- I act upon my intuition.
- I let go of judgement.
- My willpower is strong and *graceful.*

Chakra VI

Location: Third Eye (between the brows along the forehead)
Color: Indigo
Sacred Truth: *"Seek only the Truth"*

Energy:

Intelligence	Mental Body	Psychological Skills
Wisdom	Reasoning	Evaluation Skills
Intuitive Insight	Understanding	Inner Vision
Insight	World Service	Spirituality
Compassion	Mind	

Affirmations for the sixth chakra
- The world does not hold power over me.
- I choose to listen to my inside world.
- My 6th chakra is open and balanced.
- I am compassionate.
- I trust my inner voice.
- I serve my Higher Power willingly.

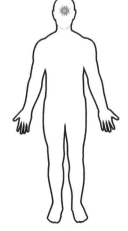

Chakra VII

Location: Crown
Color: Violet
Sacred Truth: *"Live in the present moment"*

Energy:

Spirituality	Prayer	Devotion
Grace	Visions	Hope
Mystical Connection	Prophetic Thought	True Healing
Divine Purpose	The Source of Miracles	Destiny
Transcendence	Union with the Divine	
Where the body and spirit fuse		

Affirmations for the seventh chakra
- I am.
- I am always safe.
- I follow my intuition.
- I am loved and loving.
- I am open.
- I am open to all possibilities.
- My Crown chakra is open and balanced.
- I am connected to my Higher Power.
- My spirit blesses me every day.
- I am connected with my highest good.

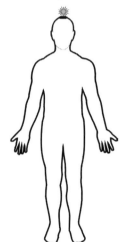

Light Bulb Moment Exercises
Aha's!

Here are some wonderful exercises that keep the light bulb moments coming. Light Bulb moments are about the life changing transformation that comes from "getting it." This is when you sit back and say, *"Oh yeah, this is why I feel this way,"* or *"I get it,"* or *"I've been stuck because of this or that, now I get it."* These *awarenesses* are your lessons in Life-School.

Journaling

Keep a journal. If your life is worth living, it's worth recording.
We learn many lessons through this process.

Here are some journaling ideas:
- Goals and dreams journal
- Gratitude journal
- Daily journal / diary
- Favorite poems and sayings
- Aha's (light bulb moments)

Forgiveness Exercises

These are VERY powerful exercises.
The first exercise can be done alone or in group.
The second exercise is done best in group.
When you are practicing alone, *read* through these exercises first and then go into meditation and *do* them.
When doing this with someone else, it's wonderful to have a facilitator read the exercise or take turns facilitating and reading.
Take your time as you sort through each person that comes into your consciousness. Allow plenty of time for the little child at the end.

Forgiveness Exercise 1

Put yourself into an Alpha state and create some type of calming preparation ...
Then,

Imagine that you are standing in a small room and, as you look down at your feet, you notice that you are wearing black shoes. You also notice that you are dressed in a black robe; you are a judge in your waiting chamber. You look up and see a door in front of you and decide to move toward it. As you walk through the door you hear the words, "All Rise," as you move to the Judge's bench. Look out into the faces of all the people in your life who have come to receive judgement from you today. You sit and pick up your gavel. Sounding it upon the desk, you hear yourself saying, "Court is in session." Those who are there now begin to line up in front of you. As they line up, you notice your spouse, partner, ex-spouse, ex-partner, mother, father, children, sisters and brothers, other relatives, teachers, boss, ex-boss, ex-lover, friends, ex-friends, business partners and associates, and anyone who has been in your life. See all of these people you know from your past. They have all come before you today to receive their judgement from you. As the first one comes up, look this person in the eyes and say to them:

I forgive you and release you, for I have looked into your heart and see you are innocent.

Continue to breathe as each person comes to you. Repeat with each one.

I forgive you and release you, for I have looked into your heart and see you are innocent.

When you have finished passing judgements upon each person, look into the very back of the room and see a small person who is coming forward. This person is YOU as a child. Have that child stand before you and look directly into his/her eyes and repeat ...

I forgive you and release you, for I have looked into your heart and see you are innocent.

When you are completed, you may return your awareness back to the room and make any notes you'd like.

Forgiveness Exercise 2

There are two basic points to this exercise:
- It is much easier to forgive someone when they say they are sorry first.
- Although difficult to understand, people do the best they can.

Make sure you are in a safe, quiet environment. Be with a person or people you trust. Hold hands if you like and face one another.

One person will read while the others are involved in the exercise.

Look into each other's eyes and read and receive these words:

Fill in the blanks with...
- Mother
- Father
- Brother/ sister
- Husband/ wife
- Perpetrator
- Or anyone else you would like to forgive

I am not your _____, but I stand in his/her place.
I represent all _____ everywhere.
I am so, so sorry.
I know that I was not always there when you needed me.

I know I did not always do and say the right things.
Deep in my soul I know these things.
I am so sorry.
I did the best I could at the time and I did not mean to harm you.
I know that seems hard to believe, but it was all I was capable of.
I love you.
I am sorry.
Please forgive me on whatever level you can so that you may begin to heal.

Make sure you have tissues around for Forgiveness Exercises.

Letter to God and Back

This exercise changed my life. It altered the way I pray and how I believe God communicates with me.

Alpha Induction or some type of calming preperation...
Then:
Write a letter **to** God. Say anything and everything you want God to hear. You can talk about ANYTHING.

When you feel complete:
Write a letter back **from** God to you. It is absolutely astonishing; the insight that seems to come from your pen to your paper is all knowing and truly the wisdom of spirit.

I do this exercise anytime I feel stuck and need a hand from Higher Guidance.

Variation:
When making a decision or feeling confused, just state:
"Dear Lord, what would you have me do?" Something will come.

What's Up Exercise

Get out your journal and write on the top of a page,
"What is working in my life?"
And write all the wonderful things in your life that ARE working well.

Then, atop another page, write:
"What is NOT working in my life?"
And list the things that are NOT working.

Take out a third page.
Write out things you can do "RIGHT NOW" that will create more of what IS working and less of what IS NOT working. This can be done in conjunction with goal setting.

Then, **DO IT!**

You can also use this exercise when trying to make a decision in life.
Figure out all the pros and cons and make your decision accordingly. Don't forget to listen to your intuition too!

Funeral Exercise

Alpha Induction or some type of calming preparation...
Then,

In your mind's eye, see yourself going to the funeral of a loved one. Picture yourself driving to the funeral parlor or chapel, parking the car, and getting out. As you walk inside the building, you notice the flowers, the soft music, you see the faces of friends and family you pass along the way. You feel the shared sorrow of loss and the joy of having known, that radiates from the hearts of all the people there.

As you walk down to the front of the room and look inside the casket, you suddenly come face to face with YOURSELF. This is YOUR funeral, many years from today. All these people have come to honor YOU, to express feelings of love and appreciation for your life.

As you take a seat and wait for the services to begin, you look at the program in your hand. There are to be four speakers.

The first is from your family, immediate and also extended ...

Children, brothers, sisters, nieces and nephews, aunts and uncles, cousins, parents, grandparents who have come from all over the country to attend.

The second speaker is one of your friends, someone who can give a sense of what you were as a person and friend.

The third speaker is from your work or profession, here to share experiences in your work.

And the fourth is from your church or some community organization where you've been involved in service.

Now think deeply.
What would you like each of these speakers to say about you and your life?
What kind of family person would you like them to remember?
Friend?
Co-worker or boss?
Community member?
What character would you like them to have seen in you?
What contributions and achievements?
Look carefully at the people around you and ask, "What difference have I made in their lives?"

Letter to Someone You Love

If today I knew that ___(so and so)___ was going to die tomorrow, what would I want him or her to know?

Paradigm Shifting Exercise

Learning about your perspective, or the lens through which you see life, can be transformational. Often, we don't even realize why we think the way we do. Actually, it comes from our personality perspective, our upbringing, environment, and experiences. It's eye opening to see some of the prejudices and concepts we have acquired.

What we think about is what we attract (right?), so for example if I think… "Women are ... catty, weak, always late, make mountains out of molehills ..." What type of women do you think I attract in my life?

If I believe women are strong, spirited, and self-motivated ... then that's the kind of women I will attract. Get it?

Societal thinking and the beliefs of our family and friends strongly affect our own beliefs. Quotes like, "Money is the root of all evil," "Real men don't cry," "You're a girl, you're not supposed to play football," can form our basic beliefs.

Try this exercise on for size. Be open-minded and write down all the feelings you have.

Men are ...	Money is ...
Women are ...	Success is ...
Mothers are ...	Having my dreams come true is ...
Fathers are ...	Leisure time is ...
Brothers are ...	Work is ...
Sisters are ...	Children are ...
Friends are ...	God is ...
Failure is ...	Old age is ...
Anger is ...	Criticism is ...
Judgements are ...	Forgiveness is ...
Work is ...	Sex is ...
Intimacy is ...	Love is ...

My health is ...
   (What do you believe about your health? – I get two colds a year. I'm always hurting myself. My parents have cancer, so I'll probably get cancer too, etc.)

Fears and Phobias
   (What do you grind into your beliefs, day after day? – I'm deathly afraid of_____. I'll never be able to face _____).

Addictions are, for example ...
   "I smoke because it reduces my stress." " I eat when I'm stressed out." "A few drinks at night won't hurt anything."

Can you think of others?

Just becoming aware of your thought patterns can be transformational.

Once you've completed the above exercise ...

See if you can take the "negative" and turn it into positive. For example, you may have been taught that money is the root of all evil, it doesn't grow on trees, you can never have enough of it, and EVERYTHING is too expensive. Shift those old wive's tales, too. "The lust for money is the root of all evil," "I use my money for the good of all mankind." "Money isn't everything, but it sure beats poverty." "It doesn't **grow** on trees, it's **made** out of trees." (You can make it fun!) "Money is only an exchange of energy." "I am so fortunate to have the money I do – I don't have to grind my own wheat, build my own roads, or mine my own salt. I am thankful for money energy."

More Paradigm Shifting

Here's an outline to see where your inner sight lies. Be truthful to yourself as you fill in the blanks.

I feel sad when I _____
I feel sad when someone else_____
I feel angry when I _____
I feel angry when someone else _____
I like to hide my emotions from others because _____
I dread the day I have to _____
When someone criticizes me it makes me feel _____
When someone yells at me, it makes me feel _____
I talk nasty to myself _____ times a day. I do this because _____
I talk nasty about others _____ times a day. I do this because _____
I think ugly thoughts _____ times a day. I do this because _____
I am afraid of _____
I think I can't_____
I won't _____
I judge _____
I worry about the past _____ times a day
I worry about the future _____ times a day
I think worry thoughts _____ a day
I know I repress my emotions about _____
I feel addicted to _____ because _____
I over-indulge in _____
I know I should prioritize about _____, but I don't.

Go over this list and decide just what you WANT from life and what you're willing to DO to change. Sanity, joy, peace, love… they're all just a thought-form away.

$100.00 Exercise

Imagine that you are only given $100.00 worth of energy each day to spend. What would you like to spend it on? What drains your energy? What gives you energy? Here are a few examples of draining energy. Imagine that each robs you of $1.00, $5.00 or even $30.00 each and every day. Is it worth it?

Worry about:
the past	the future	money	friends
family	your body	your job	the world

Could you imagine making decisions according to whether or not something or someone is stealing your energy? "I'm sorry, Mr. So-and-So, I think this relationship wouldn't work for me. You would cost me at least $25.00 a day." or "I am not spending another dime on worrying about my body image. I'll put the energy towards loving myself." Figure out your daily expenditures.

Letter to Someone You are Carrying on Your Shoulders

A few times in my life I have written letters to people who *really pissed me off*. I reamed them up and down and told them just how awful I thought they where. Thank God, my husband didn't let me send those letters, but wow, did it feel good to write them. THEY did this to me and THEY did that to me. And THEY ARE this or that. Wow! What awesome lessons. Write that (those) letter(s).

Dear so and so ...

THEN, let writing assist YOU in your healing process. Re-evaluate your situation and how you feel. Try this, instead of "You, you, you"… change it to … "When you act like this or when you do that, it makes me feel like this."

THEN, ask yourself, what is this about ME? Why does this person push my buttons? Why do I allow them to make me feel this way?

Once, when I felt betrayed by an important figure in my life, I wrote him this nasty letter that told him what was wrong with him since the day I met him. He was a role model in some ways, but the whole relationship had gotten twisted. First, I wrote him that very nasty letter. John, my husband, told me I shouldn't send it, but I was adamant. John pleaded with me to hold on to it for just a few days before I made such a harsh decision, so I did not send it, but planned to. Over the course of those few days, I began to soften up, noticing that just the right quotes and reading material were in my path (of course, about forgiveness, etc.). People did and said just the right things (all coincidences, again, of course). After several days not only did I not send the letter, I rewrote a letter to him and told him that I loved him and honored him, I was happy for whatever he wanted to do in life, that our lives were taking different courses and to go in peace, but please, stay out of my life for a while. I was sooo relieved that I didn't send that first letter. And yes, I did send the second letter. He was once an emotional drain on my energy bank. Now he's just a pleasant memory that I'm thankful for.

Another time, I had "had it" with my father, so I wrote HIM a letter. This one was very carefully structured and took a long time to write. I didn't blame him for anything in the letter, but I had to get a lifetime worth of stuff off my shoulders. I held on to the letter for some time and finally, sent it. A week or so later, my father called me, quite a novelty unto itself (he believed us kids should always make the calls). I asked him if he received the letter and he told me that he had. "So?" I asked. Then he basically told me that I was nuts and that I imagined all the stuff I wrote about. BUT, guess what? It didn't matter what he said!! I wrote the letter for ME! And I felt great!

You don't have to send the letter. You can write letters over a course of time to the same person and watch your healing processes. At the end of it all, it feels great to send a letter of love and forgiveness.

Affirmation Exercise

Affirmations work wonders ... sometimes. There often needs to be a "why" behind an affirmation and there needs to be a transformational force behind your willingness to change your mind about something. When you don't actually believe what you are affirming, try this...

Write out the affirmation, for example, I am loved.
Then, write out your disbelieving thoughts: Ya, right.
Then write it again: I am loved.
Then write out another disbelieving thought.

I've always had to DO something in order to be loved. People only love me when they WANT something from me.
    I am loved
I don't feel loved
    I am loved
My parents loved my sister more
    I am loved
My relationships in my life have often felt unloving
    I am loved
I want to be loved, but how?
    I am loved
I don't know how to be loved. I don't even know how TO love.
    I am loved
I am willing to change.
    I am loved
I'll be on the path of trying to be loved
    I am loved
My kids love me
    I am loved

I can create loving relationships in my life
> I am loved

I've always heard that in order to receive love you must be willing to give love
> I am loved

I will give love
> I am loved

I am loved
> I am loved

YAAAAHHH!!!

Etc., etc., etc.,

Keep going until you have no more excuses. All you have left is TO BE LOVED! This also helps you to find out why you don't feel loved and it gets behind the WHY of your emotions.

Rocking Chair Test

When making an important decision in life or working on personal changes, try this ...

In your mind's eye, imagine that you're eighty-five years old and you're sitting on your porch on a rocking chair overlooking your life. Sit back on the chair and rock for a while and pretend to remember when you made this particular decision or change in your life. Imagine making the decision or change, living with the rebound of it all, and playing out how your life was affected. You may want to try a different fork in the road and play out that scenario.

- How does it feel?
- Can you see how it has affected your life?
- How it has affected others around you?
- Are there aspects of your decision that makes you feel a certain way?

This exercise can help you with the emotion of *regret*. If you make a choice with the best intentions and the most information that you have at any given time, the feeling of regret can be written off. Regret can be a powerful chi robber and energy taker. The *what if's* and the *I should have's* will no longer be a part of your vocabulary, because, after all, everyone does the best they can at the time, right?

Code of Ethics

Write out a personal code of ethics. You can use many resources like the Bible, a spiritual handbook, or by emulating people you hold in the highest regard.

Write out what you KNOW to be RIGHT and then...
Follow the code...no exceptions.

Attribute Exercise

- Write out all the attributes of a person or persons you hold in high regard.
- Realize that YOU ALREADY have all these attributes, otherwise you could not recognze them.
- Recognize how and where you bring the attributes into your life.

Shape Shifting with a Partner

- You will need about an hour for this exercise. Find a partner.
- Face one another. Try to relax and keep your spine straight.
- Breathe gently and slowly through your nose, diaphragmatically.
- Gaze at one another's third eye. That's it!
- Do this for between a half an hour and an hour.
- This exercise is very powerful, and the things you see may absolutely amaze you.

Smile Exercise

Sit in a chair, spine erect, hands lightly resting on your thighs, close your eyes to center yourself for a moment, and breathe ... Now open your eyes, look up at the ceiling, think sad, depressing thoughts, and now SMILE!

This exercise just cracks me up! The first time I did it I chuckled all day. I learned two important lessons from this visualization. First, by changing your posture, you can change your mood. And second, we can control our thoughts. We are not slaves to our mind and ego.

Mirror Exercise

Get a hand held mirror and sit quietly somewhere, alone. Place the mirror in front of your face and look into your eyes ... just your eyes. Try to make no judgement or allow any emotions to be evoked yet. You might even imagine that you're looking at a stranger. Continue to gaze into your eyes and repeat these words ...

I LOVE YOU, I value you and I know there is much more to you than I see staring back at me.

Now, you may laugh, giggle, cry, get angry, or even be unable to utter the words. But, keep trying until you can say and *mean* it. (This may be no short term task).

Moving Communication Exercise in Group

According to the psychospiritual concepts of The Course In Miracles, our bodies do not communicate, only minds communicate. The purpose of this exercise is to experience this level of consciousness.

Assemble a group of people and move about in a free, open room and look at one another, one at a time, eye to eye. Stay with each person as long as it takes to to experience one another, communicate what needs to be expressed and to feel complete. Gaze into each others' eyes and experience communication through mind. There is no touching or hugging, simply move about and engage the eyes, pause until completion, and then move on to each person in the room until everyone in the group has experienced each other.

It is helpful to use soothing and relaxing music.

River of Time

Whether you believe that we are here on earth many times over, or that we live all lives, or that we only have one life but can learn from many different lifetimes of experiences, you can benefit from this exercise. You go back in time, and you may experience different times in *this* lifetime, prior lifetimes, or lessons from many lives.

First, put yourself into an alpha state using the alpha induction experience. Then... Imagine...

Before you, you see a river. It is the river of time and we shall take a trip to retrieve any lessons that we have learned that would serve a purpose now.

So, go to your canoe, grab your paddle, and begin your journey down the river. Further and further back through time.

After a while, you see a dock and decide to land. As you climb onto land, look down at your feet and see what kind of shoes you are wearing. Notice your legs and then your body. What are you wearing, who are you?

You see a path before you and decide to venture through. As you enter an opening, you see your village, city, town, or home. Notice what is happening. Notice who your people are. In what capacity do you serve in this life time? Take time to experience your people and your life here. What lessons have you learned?

When you feel complete. Head back through the path to your landing. Let us again board the canoe and paddle even further back through the river of time.

Repeat this exercise as often as feels beneficial.

During workshops we will usually do three landings and then come back to our original time and place.

Ever Changing Commitments

Commitment is a funny thing, it can be a wonderful, positive thing, or it can be burdensome and cumbersome.

Example:

If I am starting a new exercise program and I pledge to myself that I will walk one mile three times per week, it is an appropriate goal and I can commit to that. A few months later, that becomes easy and I shift my goal to walking 2 miles each time and I'd like to improve my time a little to get a better cardiovascular workout. I'm starting to love how I feel and look. A friend of mine is talking to me about doing a four-mile marathon. It sounds really fun. I'd get in terrific shape and I'd love to spend time training with my friend. If I choose to do that marathon, however, would it be appropriate for me to continue to walk? Only two miles? Would I have to make other commitments to accomplish my goals?

So, it's a new time, new goal, and I am not the same person I was a few months ago. It's OK to change my commitment.

Example:

"I married a man ten years ago and at that time I thought I could change him and we'd be happy. I have changed a lot during these years. I have taken a very different path in life and my goals are peace, freedom, joy, and happiness. We have worked hard at the marriage, but he is abusive, controlling, and is unwilling to work on our relationship and on himself. I made a commitment to our marriage, but now I want out."

So, it's a new time, I have new goals, and I am not the same person I was a few years, months, or days ago. It's OK to change my commitment.

These two scenarios sound so different, but do you see the similarities? We are ever-changing, growing, and expanding. It's OK to change your mind.

Try saying:
I revoke any commitment I have made at a lower state of mind.
I am free to choose. I am free.

Candle Ceremony

This exercise can be done alone or with a group. You will need either an outdoor fire, a fireplace, or a candle with water surrounding it or nearby. I like to put a large candle in the middle of a beautiful bowl of water.

This is a wonderful ritual done in conjunction with other personal growth exercises that incorporate work around understanding *what it is that you want in life and what you would like to let go of.*

Once you decide what you would like to let go of ... write it down on a piece of paper and ceremonially let it go by burning the paper, then place the ashes in water if you are inside. This can be very symbolic, constructive, and powerful.

Muscle Testing

Muscle testing is a remarkable tool you can use to ask your body questions and get intuitive answers. This practice is based on the fact that your body is both literal and all-knowing. There are many variations of the actual test itself, but it boils down to the body being strong when confronted with something that is good for it, and it is weak when approached with something detrimental or not as good for it.

Here's an example:
First, stretch one arm directly sideways at a 90 degree angle to your torso, hand down and arm parallel to your shoulder. Test the strength of your arm by having someone press down on the arm while you hold it strong, but not rigidly forced (imagine energy streaming out the arm straight out toward a wall).

Second, visualize a thought or ask a question. "Think of eating an entire chocolate cake." For most people, not all, this is not a great thing for the body. Test the strength of the arm again. It almost always weakens.

Third, imagine a different thought or question. "Think of eating a fresh, organic salad." If that is good for YOUR body, the strength test will be stronger.

Here's some other ways to use this:
- Name any person, place, or thing and see how it tests.
- Name any situation and test your response.
- Test your goals.
- Test an ailment or illnes. You might ask, "What is this REALLY about," and give some ideas and see how they test.

Remember though, your ego and subconscious can get in the way, so take everything with a grain of salt. If you think you are influencing the outcome through your mind, write down your thoughts or questions on a piece of paper and place them randomly in your hand, *then* ask the questions. The results may be surprising.

Goal Setting

It's very difficult to go somewhere when you don't know where you want to go. Through my experience over the years in working with thousands of people, I have found that most people who feel lost, really are. They don't know what they want. You can have a map in front of you, but it is useless if you don't know where you are or where you are going. The most successful and happy people in the world almost always have set their sight on something and went for it. They had a vision, they had a plan.
- Write a goal statement.
- Decide where you are right now.
- Decide where you want to go.
- Include a realistic time line and very specific goals.

You may want to include: friends, family, work, play, material objects, travel, education, spiritual fulfillment, and health.

- Be open to ALL possibilities. Dare to dream.
- Be ready to change your goals as you change.
- Write them out. Read them twice a day (abbreviate if necessary).
- Allow yourself to find a balance between your goals, listening to intuition and leaving things in God's hands. God helps those who help themselves.

Remember:
If you don't know where you want to go, any road will get you there!

I'd like to share my experience:

Many years ago I wrote a goal statement for a business I was involved in. Although that business did not come to fruition, my final goals did. I dreamed that my family would be healthy and happy and that we would spend quality time together. I dreamed that some day John and I would spend half the year in Florida and half in Maine. I even kept an old drawing from at least a dozen years ago with John, Sean, Shannon, and me on a boat with palm trees all around us. I wanted to spend more time at our camp in the wilderness and I now do. I dreamed that my work in the whole health community would be well accepted and that I would be busy sharing my work, directing programs, lecturing, writing, and creating audio and video tapes.

Although I took some different roads to get there, my ultimate goals have been met. As for my new goals; you're all a part of them!

Bibliography:

Benson, Herbert. *The Relaxation Response.* New York, New York: Avon, 1976

Brennan, Barbara Ann. *Hands of Light: A Guide to Healing Through the Human Energy Field.* New York: Bantam, 1987.

Bruyere, Rosalyn L. *Wheels of Light, Chakras, Auras, and the Healing Energy of the Body.* New York, N.Y.: Fireside, 1994.

A Course in Miracles. 2nd rev. ed. Set of 3 volumes., including text, teacher's manual, workbook. Found Inner Peace, 1992.

Cove, Stephen R. *The Seven Habits of Highly Effective People: Powerful Lessons in Personal Change.* New York, N.Y.: Fireside, 1990.

Farhi, Donna. *The Breathing Book: Good Health and Vitality through Essential BreathWork.* New York, N.Y.: Henry Holt and Company, 1996.

Gawain, Shatki, *Creative Visualization.* New York, N.Y.: Bantam, 1978.

Gawain, Shakti. *Living in the Light.* San Rafael, CA.: New World Library, 1986.

Hay, Louise L. *You Can Heal Yourself.* Santa Monica, CA.: Hay House, 1982.

Hendricks, Gay. *Conscious Breathing.* New York, New York: Bantam, 1995.

Jahnke, Roger. *The Healing Promise of Qi: Creating Extraordinary Wellness through Qigong and Tai Chi.* New York, N.Y.k: McGraw Hill, 2002.

Jwing-Ming, Yang. *The Root of Chinese Chi Kung, The Secrets of Chi Kung Training:* Jamaica Plains, MA.: YMAA, 1989.

Myss, Caroline. *Anatomy of the Spirit.* New York, N.Y.: Three Rivers Press, 1996.

Myss, Caroline. *Sacred Contracts, Awakening Your Divine Potential.* New York, N.Y.: Harmony Books, 2001.

Rama, Sawami and Rudolph Ballentine and Alan Hymes. *The Science of Breath, A Practical Guide.* Honesdale, PA.: Himalayan International Institute of Yoga Science and Philosophy.

Roger, John and Peter McWilliams. *You Can't Afford the Luxury of a Negative Thought, A Book for People with Any Life-Threatening Illness – Including Life.* Los Angeles, CA.: Prelude Press, 1991.

Roman, Sanaya. *Living with Joy: Keys to Personal Power and Spiritual Transformation.* Tiburon, CA.: HJ Kramer Inc., 1986.

Sky, Michael. *Breathing, Expanding your Power and Energy.* Santa Fe, N.M.: Bear & Company, 1990.

Small, Jacquelyn. *Transformers, The Artists of Self-Creation.* New York, N.Y.:Bantam, 1992

Williamson, Marianne. *A Return to Love.* New York, N.Y.: HarperCollins, 1994.

Zukav, Gary. *The Seat of the Soul.* New York, N.Y.: Fireside, 1990.

Tapes from LifeBreath Institute
By Beth Ann Bielat

"A Healthier State of Mind"
Meditation Audio

This beautifully produced audio tape takes you through a deep meditation. Guided by Beth Bielat, you will reach new levels of relaxation. Beth has taken special care to create a pace that anyone can follow and a sound that totally enhances your journey. This meditation is intended to leave you feeling energized, vital and inspired. Includes a bonus of 30 minutes "music only" side two for use as a background during work, drive-time or sleep. (Music composed by Steve MacLean)

Cassette Tape .... $11.95 plus shipping
CD .... $14.95 plus shipping

"LifeBreath Style Tai Chi / Chi Kung"

In this professionally produced videotape, Beth leads you through easy-to-follow movements and breathing techniques that leave you feeling energized, balanced and peaceful. Learn to enhance stamina, improve balance and maximize your life energy. Beth has refined these techniques based on over thirty-five years experience as a recognized Master of Martial Arts. *LifeBreath Style Tai Chi / Chi Kung* is for people of all ages and abilities. With the beautiful scenery of the Florida Keys with the Atlantic Ocean and palm trees as a backdrop, learn how to enhance your Physical, Emotional, Mental and Spiritual well being. With the sounds of musician Steve MacLean as a background, you're sure to enjoy this beneficial video guide for years to come.

Video Tape or DVD .... $24.95 plus shipping

"A Guided LifeBreath Session and Chakra Attunement"

For thousands of years, sages of ancient civilizations have used the powerful science and inner art of breathing to master the human conditions of fear and illness and for attaining spiritual enlightenment. They discovered that through breathing, they had direct access to the divine energy of the universe. Breathing is the very key to our Physical, Emotional, Mental and Spiritual well being. Understanding your breathing is extremely beneficial and transformational. Practicing the LifeBreath Technique and aligning your energy centers in this wonderfully guided audio tape will help bring you physical rejuvenation, mental clarity, emotional balance and spiritual fulfillment. (Music composed by Steve MacLean)

Cassette Tape .... $11.95 plus shipping
CD .... $14.95 plus shipping

To Order: LifeBreath Institute
PO Box 262
Casco, Maine 04015

207-627-7170
lifebreathbeth@hotmail.com

About the Author

Beth Bielat is a nationally acclaimed fitness professional, a member of The World Karate Union Hall of Fame, founder of LifeBreath Institute, co-owner and co-founder of Bushido Karate Dojo and Fitness Center and a thirty-three year veteran in Holistic Health.

She resides with her husband and two children in Casco, Maine six months each year and travels to Tavernier, Florida the other half year. Her children attend college at the University of New Hampshire. Her husband is a Master Guide and Fishing Captain in both Maine and Florida. Beth teaches classes and workshops and creates retreats around breathwork, martial arts and physical, emotional, mental, and spiritual, well-being.

Beth can be reached at:

LifeBreath Institute
PO Box 262
Casco, Maine 04015
207-627-7170

Beth Bielat
117 Westminster Dr.
Tavernier, Florida 33070
305-852-5039

lifebreathbeth@hotmail.com